IAN KELLY

Ian Kelly's previous works include the historical biographies *Casanova* (Sunday Times Biography of the Year, 2008), *Mr Foote's Other Leg; Comedy, Tragedy and Murder in Georgian London* (Winner, Theatre Book of the Year, 2013), *Beau Brummell* (shortlisted for the Marsh Commonwealth Biography Prize), *Cooking for Kings, A Life of Antonin Carême* (Radio 4 Book of the Week), and the life of Vivienne Westwood, co-written with Dame Vivienne. As a dramatist, Ian's stage adaptation of the Carême biography *Cooking for Kings* ran Off-Broadway in 2004 and 2006. *Beau Brummell* was adapted as a BBC film with Simon Bent and starring Hugh Bonneville and James Purefoy. Ian has written for *The New York Times, Sunday Times, Telegraph, TLS, Men's Health, Gastronomica* and *Food Arts Magazine*, of which he is Contributing Editor. He wrote and originated the Film Education study series *Shakespeare Cinema*.

As an actor, film work includes *Harry Potter and the Deathly Hallows Part I* and *Part II* as Hermione's father, *Howards End, Creation, In Love and War, Closed* and the Russian films *Admiral Kolchak* and Alexei Balabanov's *War* (Best Actor Nomination, Montreal Film Festival).

Theatre work includes *The Pitmen Painters* (National Theatre, Broadway, West End and Newcastle Live; Performance of the Year, NE Culture Awards), *A Busy Day* (West End, Bristol Old Vic), *Arcadia* (Manchester), *Cooking for Kings* and *Beau Brummell* (US premieres, Off-Broadway), *Henry V* and *Twelfth Night* with the English Shakespeare Company and seasons with, amongst others, Theatr Clwyd and Salisbury Playhouse.

Television work includes *Downton Abbey, Sensitive Skin, In a Land of Plenty, Cold Lazarus, Silent Witness, Drop the Dead Donkey, Time Trumpet, Catherine Cookson's The Moth, Just William, Underworld*.

Ian grew up on Merseyside, in the States and near Bristol. He read History at Trinity H⸃   .ip to UCLA's F   e, Film, Televi⸃

Ian Kelly

MR FOOTE'S OTHER LEG

Based on *Mr Foote's Other Leg;*
Comedy, Tragedy and Murder in Georgian London
by Ian Kelly

Introduced by the author

NICK HERN BOOKS
London
www.nickhernbooks.co.uk

A Nick Hern Book

Mr Foote's Other Leg first published in Great Britain as a paperback original in 2015 by Nick Hern Books Limited, The Glasshouse, 49a Goldhawk Road, London W12 8QP

Adapted for the stage from *Mr Foote's Other Leg; Comedy, Tragedy and Murder in Georgian London* published in 2012 by Picador PanMacmillan Books

Mr Foote's Other Leg copyright © 2015 Ian Kelly
Introduction copyright © 2015 Ian Kelly
Some of the introductory material first published in *Mr Foote's Other Leg; Comedy, Tragedy and Murder in Georgian London* © Ian Kelly (Picador PanMacmillan, 2012). Winner of the Theatre Book of the Year Award from the Society of Theatre Research, 2013. Reproduced with the publisher's permission.

Ian Kelly has asserted his right to be identified as the author of this work

Cover image by Dewynters; back cover image © Pan Macmillan

Designed and typeset by Nick Hern Books, London
Printed and bound in Great Britain by CPI Group (UK) Ltd

A CIP catalogue record for this book is available from the British Library

ISBN   978 1 84842 507 1

CAUTION   All rights whatsoever in this play are strictly reserved. Requests to reproduce the text in whole or in part should be addressed to the publisher.

Amateur Performing Rights   Applications for performance, including readings and excerpts, by amateurs in the English language throughout the world should be addressed to the Performing Rights Manager, Nick Hern Books, The Glasshouse, 49a Goldhawk Road, London W12 8QP, *tel* +44 (0)20 8749 4953, *email* info@nickhernbooks.co.uk, except as follows:

Australia: Dominie Drama, 8 Cross Street, Brookvale 2100, *fax* (2) 9938 8695, *email* drama@dominie.com.au

New Zealand: Play Bureau, PO Box 9013, St Clair, Dunedin 9047, *tel* (3) 455 9959, *email* info@playbureau.com

South Africa: DALRO (pty) Ltd, PO Box 31627, 2017 Braamfontein, *tel* (11) 712 8000, *fax* (11) 403 9094, *email* theatricals@dalro.co.za

United States of America and Canada: Independent Talent Group Ltd, see details below

Professional Performing Rights   Applications for performance by professionals in any medium and in any language throughout the world (and amateur and stock performances in the United States of America and Canada) should be addressed to Independent Talent Group Ltd, 40 Whitfield Street, London W1T 2RH, *tel* +44 (0)20 7636 6565

No performance of any kind may take place unless a licence has been obtained. Applications should be made before rehearsals begin. Publication of this play does not necessarily indicate its availability for performance.

'To stand in the ill-lit backstage, slightly to the side of a fully knowable truth, is the business that a biographer and an actor share.'

Mr Foote's Other Leg, the Biography of Samuel Foote

A Short Prologue from the Author at the Footlights

'Dates,' remarked the Georgian courtesan Harriette Wilson, 'make ladies nervous and stories dull.' Not everything in this play happened in the order I have it happen here, or the place, or time. Or, to misquote Morecambe and Wise, here are all the main facts, just not necessarily in the right order. If you want the proper chronology and the whole and ridiculously true story, to the best of my abilities to discover it, there is a book which shares the title of this play, a biography of Samuel Foote. This play is a free adaptation of it, so foremost thanks are due to all those who either read the book or heard about Foote and said 'This should be on stage' – a remark which at the time, I'd have to say, I took as an anxiety that perhaps this story was just too preposterous to be a non-fiction book at all...

The biography of Samuel Foote, one-legged comedy superstar of the Georgian stage, took me on a fascinating research journey through the Hunterian, Huntington and Wellcome libraries, the archives of the Garrick Club and the Lord Chamberlain's papers. But in adapting it for the stage I have striven to put across the *spirit* of Foote – one of the most extraordinary men ever to have worked in the theatre – as much as the factual detail of his bizarre career. At the same time I wanted to express some of the style of the Georgian age – a period I love – but for a modern audience, and therefore the scabrous, sexually knowing underbelly of the Augustan Age is also represented here in all its four-letter, rakehelly, occasionally rancid ridiculousness – and lack of political correctness. For this I make no apology. But I will confess to a few major wranglings of date or fact, in case any of this bothers you – though the remarkable thing really is that nearly everything you will see on stage or read in this play is true: from the murder of Mr Hallam by Charles Macklin to the hugger-mugger burial of Foote near Poets' Corner. However,

Foote's unanaesthetised leg amputation was performed in
February 1766 by William Bromfeild, another Royal Surgeon,
not John Hunter and did not take place on the stage of the
Haymarket, but at a house party in one of the aristocratic
Delaval family estates – probably Methley Hall in Yorkshire. It
happened after a fall from a 'mettlesome steed' owned by the
then Duke of York, not, as I have it in the play, by his elder
brother George III. Both princes were great admirers of the
theatre, and indeed of Foote and his friends David Garrick and
Peg Woffington – who often arranged publicity-serving wagers
– but the royal brothers have been conflated into one character
in the play. Benjamin Franklin knew them all, but was not
always in London when and where I place him, nor
experimenting with Hunter in quite the ways I have them. It
was Foote, not Lord Chesterfield, who first made the joke about
embracing principles and mistresses, though both of them may
have been quoting Mirabeau quoting an earlier French comedy.
And so on. In comedy, as in music, it is often very difficult to
ascertain where and when the notes first came together, and I
have had to let go of my instincts as a historian some of the
time in the interests of what I wanted to say about the theatre,
then and now.

Most pertinently perhaps, Frank Barber, one of the great semi-
lost figures of British Black history, who went on to work for Dr
Johnson and was known well by Foote (and who did go missing
for some months during his time in London, to the great distress
of Dr Johnson), never worked for Samuel Foote as his dresser.
The man whose evidence nearly sent Foote to prison or to the
gallows, 'Roger the Footman' as he became known in the
irreverent London papers, was a valet and coachman in Foote's
employ at the Haymarket called John Sangster. He is
occasionally referred to as 'black', but this is much more likely
at the time to have been an assessment of his character than his
race. Nevertheless, many of London's substantial Black
population in Georgian times seem to have worked on the
fringes of respectability – in the theatre, music and indeed the
sex trade. They had an uneasy relationship with the law. Lord
Mansfield, who ruled in the case against Foote and indeed also

against the bigamous Duchess of Kingston, declared in 1772 that slavery was 'odious and immoral' – but this did not altogether clear up whether or not it was illegal. Many men and women of African descent did live in Georgian London – it is controversial quite how many but it could have been many thousands – having been 'granted' their freedom by 'owners', and having themselves baptised in the belief that, as Christians, they could not be held as slaves. Francis Barber, who was the main beneficiary of Samuel Johnson's will and seems to have been Britain's first Black schoolmaster, has long intrigued me as a character. He is in this play in fictionalised form for a number of reasons, not least of which is to underline that *Mr Foote's Other Leg*, the play, is a *story*, as well as *history*: a discourse on eighteenth-century lost voices, lost reputations, forgotten histories, and self-determination – sexual and otherwise. And because one of the first things that ever made me laugh about Foote was his attempt to turn *Othello* into a comedy.

Much else, and many of the lines of this play, come direct from the archive or from Foote's own plays and collected 'bons mots', or indeed from Foote's own deliberate satirising of the works of his contemporaries: Fielding, Addison, Johnson, Pope and his friend David Garrick. Some are jokes and stories that were told to me by actors who knew of Foote – the oral history of The Green Room – and these I wanted to include, now freed from the need to footnote (sic) because, when it was suggested my book ought to be a play, I knew I wanted to write a love letter to the theatre, dedicated to its unsung heroes – including producers and stage management – and forgotten performers. Many of the incidents in the play – from royal visits backstage to arguments and love affairs in dressing rooms – are written from experience after years of working in the London theatre. In some regards, little has changed in two hundred years. More than this, it has long seemed to me that the theatre in the eighteenth century served as a prism though which our Georgian forebears saw themselves, rocked as they were by revolutions scientific, sexual and political. And John Hunter, as one example, returned over and over again to the theatre as a metaphor in his scientific hypotheses, knowing much about it, and many of its practitioners, on the most intimate level. So to write about the theatre, for and in the theatre, was the task I set myself, though this sort of discussion on stage is of course hardly unfamiliar.

Appropriately enough, then, this all began backstage. The play and book were born of a conversation at the National Theatre with Lee Hall. We were working together on Lee's wonderful play *The Pitmen Painters* when we first talked about Sam Foote. Like many who trawl in eighteenth-century studies, I had heard of Foote, long before even my research towards a biography of Casanova, whose notes on his 1763 London year included mention of bumping into Foote, quite literally, on the Haymarket. So the journey that takes us from page to stage, actually began in the theatre, and I must thank first of all my good friend Lee Hall and my publisher and friend Paul Baggaley of Picador PanMacmillan for having insane faith in the story, and in me, and the whole team who brought the book together, notably Kris Doyle at Picador and my literary agents Ivan Mulcahy and Cathy King. Further thanks are due to the Wellcome Trust and the Huntington Library for grants towards the research and writing of both the biography of Foote and this play, but also to friends in the theatre and theatre-history who have advised and cajoled and nurtured this into being: Andy Holland, the finest script doctor I know; the exceptional Lisa Hilton and Sasha Damianovsky, who were particularly helpful; along with a host of new friends in Tim Phillips' Writers' Group in Los Angeles, but especially Rich Schiff, Robin Weingert, Annie LaGravenese, Joe Spano, Victor Bumbalo and Arvind Ethan David, who suffered a much, much longer version of the play, and one played largely in American accents. Thanks also to early-readers Lindsey Clay, Matt White, Milo Twomey, Kate Bassett and especially to the wonderful actress Claire Davies and the cast at Hampstead, who have been, already, more illuminating and instructive than I could ever have hoped. Giles Duley, as well as Dr Johnson, has kindly contributed various 'depedition' and other jokes; some further quips, suggested to me over the months, turned out rather marvellously to have been first stropped by Foote himself, and misquoted down the

centuries. But most profound thanks must go to Michael
Codron and Richard Eyre. It was Sir Michael who, having read
the book, sent it to Sir Richard as a seventieth-birthday present
and expressed the thought to him, and later to me, that it ought
to be a play. Such was the original spur to adapt. This is
dedicated to Sir Michael, another Worcester man like Foote,
whose wit, warmth and wise counsel nurtured this towards the
stage, where I had always hoped it might find footfall. This
playscript goes to press before rehearsals have ended, so I have
every faith that the play will change further and for the better –
and if nothing else, as we are always admonished in the theatre,
will end up faster and funnier. I hope so.

The process from biography to play can be perplexing. It is all
the more so, perhaps, when both biography and play are the
fruit of parallel research, partly, but only partly, to do with the
theatre itself. Foote's name first came to prominence in
Georgian England as a result of the true-crime bestseller he
penned about the grisly murder of his uncle by his other uncle
after many decades of wrangling over a family inheritance. It's
a fascinating story, and Foote holds his place in the history of
crime writing as well as celebrity notoriety, but it was clear that
the mountain of research that generated the opening quarter of
the book was fruitless in dramatic terms. Or will make for
another play. Nevertheless, the ghosts of that murder, and the
trail it set me around the anatomising of criminals and
celebrities, speak still in the opening scene and in the
importantly grisly business of what Hunter actually did, since
one central concern shared by both book and play is to do with
the anatomising of celebrities and the linked origins of modern
theatre culture and modern medicine. My first memories are of
my father's specimen collections – he is a veterinary pathologist
– and of post-mortems: possibly not the sort of thing small
children are encouraged to witness these days. But the radical
anti-sentimentality that drives forward all science, all free
thinking and of course all medicine represents one gift of the
Age of Reason, worth celebrating and protecting. The history of
medicine has been a recurrent theme in my books, partly as the
eighteenth century tends to furnish a great deal of evidence but

very little accurate understanding, partly because what fascinates me often about history is the delving into genesis myths. The new discussions on the meaning of self in this era – in philosophy and the arts and in politics – had their corollary in medicine and in what would now be termed neuroscience. Though Hunter was wrong in many areas, he was prescient elsewhere and laid a great deal of the groundwork towards a modern understanding of medical methodology and the corporeality of the 'mind'. That he used the theatre as metaphor in this discussion linked his world directly to that of Foote's; both addressing in their different ways the new understandings of self, or free thought, and ultimately of mental ill-health. The past is never so foreign a country as it is in its relationship with pain and with the nearness of death, and one vital reason for telling this story, as book and now as play, was to address the heroism of Foote and of the scientific professions at the time, battling as they did prejudices which would now largely be considered ignorant, but at enormous personal cost. I am indebted to the work of Wendy Moore and Will Storr, and the guidance of Simon Chaplin, formerly of the Hunterian, for initial inspiration towards this aspect of the play: though for the deliberate updating of some of the terminology and argument I take full responsibility.

***

Foote holds an intriguing place in our collective history, not just the theatre's. 'Why should a man once famous enough to be represented by a simple icon – a foot – be forgotten now?' was one question both book and play seek to explain. A coiner of comedies for one-legged actors and the original celebrity-impressionist, Foote must own some of the authorship of his own obscurity. Added to this, Foote's famous name became a whispered one in the immediate aftermath of the trial that ended his career. Neither, it should be said, are his plays very stage-worthy any more. His thirty-odd comedy 'afterpieces' relied heavily on topical jokes and the inwit of a celebrity-impressionist and only a few remained popular into the nineteenth century. If his ribaldry sings out still in the names of his creations – Sir Archy McSarcasm, the priapic Harry Humper or one-legged Sir Luke Limp – their lines, regrettably, now ring hollow. To me anyway. There are many real Foote lines in the play, but they are generally not from his plays.

The play, like the book, is instead an attempted exploration of mid-eighteenth-century London's fascination with the theatre, viewed from the unique vantage point of a troubled, one-legged master of ceremonies, a man of breathtakingly catholic experience and larrikin wit; a tale told by an actor. How Samuel Foote lost his leg and thereby gained a royal licence for a theatre – one of only three such Theatres Royal in the whole history of the London stage – is one subject of this play. How a man of such singular anatomy could be at the centre of one of the most sensational buggery trials in British history – a subject of hilarious conjecture at the time, wiping the American Declaration of Independence off the London papers for many months – turns out to be a story less of perplexing balance than of shocking brutality and prejudice. But it is also the story of a comic, and the play even more than the book seeks to reflect that, and pay tribute to Foote with the sound he most favoured in his theatre, that of laughter. Foote's story has, of course, some resonance with the scandal that ended Oscar Wilde's career: his fame, personality and tragic trajectory illuminating uncomfortable truths about his era, and his posthumous allure inextricably linked to his downfall. But it is the question of *why* Londoners should turn their attention to scandal, celebrity and laughter through 1776, when they might have paid closer attention to events in America, that also fascinates, as well as forging both backdrop and cacophonous noises-off to Foote's tragicomedy. Appropriately enough then this is the story also of the man who seemingly coined the phrase 'Tea Party' – a rallying cry at Boston harbour in 1773 – though Foote used it as an irreverent circumvention of the London censors: he sold tickets for tea, and added a scurrilous satire on the side. So now, finally, he is having the last laugh, as the unexpected godfather of an American reactionary movement, which, given his other reputation as sexual deviant and reckless transvestite satirist, would surely give him cause to smirk.

From his Westminster grave, Foote may or may not relish his reputation as a sort of gay martyr. Only here and there, in his attacks on Methodism, nabobs and the medical establishment, did his comedy pack political punch, and it would be wildly anachronistic to have him enunciate a fully modern understanding of sexual tolerance or (trans) gender politics. And yet his triumphs, though personal, are not without their political significance. Whatever the odds stacked against him, and there were many even before the amputation and its effect upon his mental health, Foote turned things to his own account and to comedy. His daring, his refusal to bow to convention and to domestic or artistic safety, make him still commanding of our attention. More than this, both book and play represent an exploration of Samuel Foote the 'celebrity' in an age and in a city where the idea, it is argued, originates. Spectators in Georgian London became enchanted with performers: Peg Woffington and Kitty Clive, Garrick and Foote, all of them painted by the new celebrity portraitists and all of them beginning to manipulate anecdotes about their private lives that helped create an aura of availability, not just sexual, allowing audience and readership a fantastical journey into imagined lives. Samuel Foote launched himself with a tale of horrific murder from the unique position of a family member. People thought they knew him because they knew *of* him, even before they saw him on stage.

The loss of his leg, and the projection therefore of a despoiled masculinity, as a limping icon of pain and accident – two key ingredients in comedy – made him all the more fascinating as a star, caught, as it were, in the act of falling. Finally there was the scandal-palled demise, when, for reasons possibly related to his mental health, he pushed too hard against the establishment, or picked, in Elizabeth Chudleigh and 'Roger' Sangster, the wrong foes, and became an object of widespread opprobrium and, for some, 'the opposite of a man'. If anything is instantly recognisable in the story of Sam Foote, it is the creation of the modern trope of the celebrity destroyed, the star trammeled in the mud, who then, ideally, has some comeback either in life, or after death – though Foote, of course, did not. For some, the attacks upon a famous actor, with charges of homosexuality and of sexual assault, make Foote a sort of martyr irrespective of the veracity of either 'charge'. For us still, in thrall to the evolving culture of the famous, he is uniquely placed in the tragicomic business of stardom and at its birth: a body of evidence, in and of himself, that we are as drawn to the pain of celebrity as to its glister.

Ian Kelly,
September 2015

The Historical Characters in *Mr Foote's Other Leg*
on and offstage – in alphabetical order

The real **Frank Barber** (*c*. 1742–1801) was born into slavery
on a sugar plantation in Jamaica, came to England as a boy and
went on to work as a household servant for Dr Samuel Johnson.
For some years he worked elsewhere, including a period spent
serving in the navy, but Samuel Foote's footman, sometimes
described as 'black', was in fact called John Sangster. Of the
many thousands of Blacks known to have lived in Georgian
London, some 'freed' ex-slaves, many worked in the theatre and
music industries. When Johnson died, he left the bulk of his
estate to Barber, who went to live in Johnson's native Lichfield
and even briefly worked there as a schoolmaster.

Isaac Bickerstaffe (1733–1812?), homosexual Anglo-Irish
playwright, librettist and former page to Lord Chesterfield,
Bickerstaffe collaborated with Thomas Arne and Samuel Foote,
among others, for ventures at Drury Lane and Covent Garden,
but fled England in 1772, never to return, after a scandal
involving a guardsman in a London park.

**Elizabeth Chudleigh, Duchess of Kingston, Countess of
Bristol** (1720–88), famed beauty, fortune-hunter, scandal-
monger or proto-feminist victim of a misogynist society,
depending on your point of view or that of the coffee-house
gossips of Hogarth's London, 'The Chudleigh' was the most
infamous woman in Georgian England as a result of her trial for
bigamy before her peers in the House of Lords. She was found
guilty. Sam Foote wrote her into a comedy, banned by the Lord
Chamberlain, as 'Lady Kitty Crocodile' and her consequent
animus lead to Foote's 'outing' in the popular press, his name
and face gracing the frontispiece of a scabrous attack she paid

to have published called 'Sodom and Onan'. His trial for sodomitical assault followed close upon her trial, in 1776. He was acquitted but never recovered.

Kitty Clive (1711–85), leading lady at Drury Lane, soprano, comedienne and famed beauty; her impressive dramatic range encompassed Delilah in the premiere of Handel's *Samson* to bawdy comic maids opposite Foote, and spanned forty years from the foundations of Garrick's first company to retirement in Twickenham; supported by her admirer Horace Walpole.

'Mother' Douglas (*c*. 1700–61), known as the Empress of the Bawds, the Scottish Jenny Douglas was a St James's prostitute by the time she was seventeen, a brothel-owner by her mid-thirties, an intimate of Earl FitzWilliam, the Duke of Cumberland and Rear Admiral Holmes among others and notorious by her fifties as the inspiration for Mrs Cole, the brothel madam in John Cleland's *Fanny Hill; The Memoirs of a Woman of Pleasure*. In Foote's *The Minor*, Mrs Cole was made flesh on stage by Foote himself, who had, in drag, a marked resemblance to the ageing courtesan. Hogarth knew well Douglas's Covent Garden bordello, the former King's Head in the piazza, as did Foote. She equipped it with fashionably rococo interiors and running water and also sold her own-brand condoms manufactured by Jacobs of the Strand, presented in a silk bag 'with a ribbon round it'.

Prince Edward Augustus, Duke of York (1739–67), younger, blonder, duller brother of George III and briefly heir to the British throne, Prince 'Ned' had a lifelong interest in the theatre, even appearing as Lothario in Rowe's *The Fair Penitent*. His connection to the slightly older Mexborough-Delaval set brought Foote into contact first with him and with Elizabeth Chudleigh, at Kingston House, and later with the fateful riding accident in 1766.

Sir John Fielding (1721–80), blind magistrate, brother of the
more famous Henry; he took over as magistrate at Bow Street
on his brother's death in 1754 and was consequently presiding
when John Sangster laid his deposition against Foote in 1776.
Called as witness in the trial, Sir John claimed to be able to
recognise three thousand criminals by voice alone, and judged
character by verbal testimony. He did not hesitate to believe that
Sangster's tale was worthy of investigation.

Samuel Foote (1720–77) was a comic dramatist, actor,
impressionist and theatre manager, originally from Truro. He
first came to fame in Georgian London as a crime writer,
penning a bestselling pamphlet about the murder of his own
uncle by his other uncle. He parried his notoriety into a hugely
successful stage career, often in transvestite roles, that was
nearly ended in 1766 when his leg had to be amputated –
unanaesthetised – after a riding accident. One of the most
recognised names of the eighteenth century, Foote's reputation
was destroyed by a sensational trial that effectively eclipsed in
the London papers America's Declaration of Independence.
Original Patentee of the Theatre Royal, Haymarket, originator
of the 'matinee', and of the term 'Tea Party' to indicate a
political satire. On being accused of one-legged sexual assault
upon an employee, 'Roger the Footman', he is said to have
quipped, 'Sodomite? I'll not stand for it.' He is buried
somewhere near Poets' Corner in Westminster Abbey.

Benjamin Franklin (1706–90), a renowned polymath, Franklin
was a leading author, printer, political theorist, scientist,
inventor, and diplomat but also lover of the theatre and music.
As a scientist, he was a major figure in the Enlightenment and
the history of physics for his discoveries and theories regarding
electricity. He lived in London at various times throughout his
life in a house on Craven Street, just off the Strand, which still
exists today. His inventions, many dating from his years living
at Craven Street, included lightning rods, bifocals and a glass
harmonica, played upon by Samuel Foote among others.

David Garrick (1717–79) was an English actor, playwright, theatre manager and producer who influenced nearly all aspects of theatrical practice through his lifetime. He was the central figure in the revivification of Shakespeare's reputation in the eighteenth century. Originally from Lichfield, Garrick was a pupil and friend of Dr Samuel Johnson, and travelled when they first came to London to seek their fortunes. Garrick went on to run Drury Lane Theatre for twenty-nine years, as both friend and rival to Samuel Foote, his main competition at the Haymarket. Even Garrick's close friend Samuel Johnson had to admit that, of the two, Foote had 'the greater range of wit'. Garrick's Shakespeare Jubilee of 1769 established the first (temporary) theatre in Stratford-upon-Avon dedicated to the works of its most famous son.

Prince George, later George III (1738–1820) inherited the throne from his grandfather George II in 1760. As princes, he and his younger brother the Duke of York were frequent theatre-goers, having been brought up at Leicester House on what is now Leicester Square – and mounting amateur theatrical evenings with the Delaval family and their friend Samuel Foote. It was the Duke's horse that threw Sam Foote, leading to his leg amputation, but as a result, Foote successfully lobbied the royal brothers for a Theatre Royal licence for his theatre, the Haymarket. As King, George III was unexpectedly supportive of Samuel Foote during his 1776 trial, ordering two Royal Command Performances at the Haymarket, which he attended with his wife, Queen Charlotte.

George Frideric Handel (1685–1759) spent most of his career in London, a wildly successfully composer of baroque operas, oratorios and anthems, becoming well known for his royal and state commissions for the Hanoverian Court as well as the Coronation Anthem *Zadok the Priest*. His *Messiah* was written in support of the Coram Hospital for Foundlings. He has some place in the history of public art and music having premiered works at Vauxhall Gardens, for instance the Royal Fireworks Music, for a commercial audience. He was granted a full stage funeral at Westminster Abbey.

John Hunter (1728–93) was a Scottish surgeon, one of the most distinguished scientists of his day along with his brother William. He was an early advocate of careful observation and scientific method in medicine and is frequently described as the Father of Modern Surgery. He set up his own anatomy school in London and a museum, now known as the Hunterian, a collection of anatomical specimens and curiosities. A close friend of Sam Foote, he also treated him in his decline, and advised the surgeon, William Bromfeild, who conducted Foote's leg amputation. He appears to have designed for Foote a semi-articulated prosthesis which was constructed by the puppet makers of Covent Garden. Appointed surgeon to the King in 1776 and Surgeon General in 1790.

Samuel Johnson (1709–84), critic, Shakespeare scholar, essayist, lexicographer, depressive and possible Tourette's sufferer, he came to London from Lichfield with David Garrick in 1737. Author of *The Dictionary of the English Language* (1755) and friend to many, including Foote, whom he described as 'irresistible'.

Charles Macklin (1699–1797), born Cathal Mac-Lochlainn in Ulster, Macklin made his acting reputation under his Anglicised name and pioneered a new stage naturalism in London and Dublin. His Shylock is said to have prompted Alexander Pope to remark, 'This is the Jew that Shakespeare drew.' Macklin is also famous for killing a man in a fight over a wig at the Theatre Royal, Drury Lane, after which he was tried for murder. He later founded Britain's first drama school.

Joshua Reynolds (1723–92), friend of Foote and fellow West Country arriviste, he was assistant to the portraitist Thomas Hudson when he and Foote first met in the early 1740s. Reynolds later travelled in Italy and France and was not permanently back in London until 1753, like Foote. He painted the same 'celebrities' Foote parodied, from Elizabeth Chudleigh to David Garrick. First President of the Royal Academy.

Jack Sangster (*c*. 1751–?), country-born stable boy who rose to become second coachman in the household of Samuel Foote and occasional footman at the villa at Fulham; previously in the employ of Dr Fordyce of Soho. Wrongly named around London and in one ballad as 'Roger' the footman, and described as 'black' though this may or may not have been a racial description. He is represented in the play by the fictionalised character of Frank Barber.

John Wesley (1703–91), Anglican evangelist and preacher; with his brother Charles and the preacher George Whitefield, credited as a founding father of Methodism.

Peg Woffington (1717?–60), Margaret 'Peg' Woffington was the most famous Irish actress in Georgian London. A child star in her native Dublin – she played Polly Peachum in *The Beggar's Opera* aged only eleven – she became the leading lady of Theatre Royal at Smock Alley, before moving to London, where she lived openly with her lover David Garrick, sharing 'digs' on Bow Street, Covent Garden, rented off Charles Macklin. At one time, Samuel Foote shared the house too. Her attack on fellow actress George Anne Bellamy, onstage, with a prop-knife, became the subject of Foote's satire. Famous for her 'breeches' roles as well as her wit and sexual candour, Mrs Woffington's image was sold in print shops and even as ceramics. The most famous image of her hangs in the Garrick Club, in which she holds a miniature traditionally taken to be David Garrick.

Johann Zoffany (1733–1810), German painter, mainly successful in London, founding member of the Royal Academy, he frequently painted the new 'celebrities' of the era, especially those associated with the theatre. Two of his paintings of Foote hung in Foote's Suffolk Street house that is now the back of the Theatre Royal, Haymarket.

Mr Foote's Other Leg was first performed at Hampstead Theatre, London, on 21 September 2015 (previews from 14 September) with the following cast:

SAMUEL FOOTE	Simon Russell Beale
PEG WOFFINGTON	Dervla Kirwan
DAVID GARRICK	Joseph Millson
JOHN HUNTER	Forbes Masson
FRANK BARBER	Micah Balfour
MRS GARNER	Jenny Galloway
PRINCE GEORGE, *later* GEORGE III	Ian Kelly
CHARLES MACKLIN/ BENJAMIN FRANKLIN	Colin Stinton
ELIZABETH CHUDLEIGH	Sophie Bleasdale
HALLAM	Joshua Elliott

Director	Richard Eyre
Designer	Tim Hatley
Lighting Designer	Peter Mumford
Sound Designer	John Leonard
Casting Director	Cara Beckinsale

MR FOOTE'S OTHER LEG

Ian Kelly

Characters
SAMUEL FOOTE
PEG WOFFINGTON
DAVID GARRICK
JOHN HUNTER
FRANK BARBER
MRS GARNER
PRINCE GEORGE
CHARLES MACKLIN
BENJAMIN FRANKLIN
MISS CHUDLEIGH
HALLAM
And STAGE-HANDS, EQUERRY

The play is set in London in the mid-eighteenth century.

Note

In one scene only is the actor playing Foote required to have his leg 'strapped up'.

John Hunter designed Foote a functioning semi-articulated prosthesis, which appeared, largely, leg-like or, for the purposes of the stage, like a leg in callipers.

This text went to press before the end of rehearsals and so may differ slightly from the play as performed.

ACT ONE

Scene One

Hunter's Anatomy Museum.

In the semi-darkness FRANK, *a Black man, and an older woman,* MRS GARNER, *enter with a sedan-carriage light and candle. They are searching for something. She moves stiffly, and has to sit from time to time, but they search with urgency and speak in loud whispers.*

FRANK. Is there – is there somebody there? Is there – Who's there?

MRS GARNER. Oh – ooh – I've got it: 'Friend to the King and liegeman to the Dane'?

FRANK. What?

MRS GARNER. Time out of joint. Something rotten in the state –

FRANK. What? No. Shh.

They listen.

There's somebody here.

They light a chandelier and raise it, throwing more light on an Anatomy Museum: body parts in jars – as much a gallery of curios as a medical display.

MRS GARNER. Not as could answer you, Mr Frank. Can we not go back to the theatre, Mr Frank? Sweet heavens. I'd have to say I have had better nights with you. Giddier. Not many odder. There was the night Mr Garrick's wig caught fire, that was an odd night... and the time Mrs Bellamy's waters broke at the curtain call... as Juliet...

FRANK.... must have been alarming for Romeo... and the audience...

MRS GARNER.... and for the orchestra. No, I've had some strange nights, Mr Frank, but nothing quite as... well... as dark, Mr Frank, begging your pardon. I've never in all my sainted days seen such a charnel house of horrors – and I've seen some dodgy productions, I can tell you.

FRANK (*reads*). 'The development of the human child, in uterine', dear God.

FRANK *illuminates a row of babies in fetal positions in large display jars of clear liquid.*

MRS GARNER. Poor little bastards. They've got to teach though, haven't they? Doctors will be schooled. Though what I really object to is their charging box office. I mean these here is cheaper than actors. By far. More animated in some cases. It's unfair competition, Mr Frank, I say. Mind, there's a shelf full of cocks over here –

FRANK. What?

MRS GARNER. Maypoles, pizzles, percies, yard arms.

FRANK. Yes, Mrs Garner, me hear you.

MRS GARNER. A veritable parliament of members, Mr Frank, all constituencies. Even one of your persuasion, Mr Frank –

FRANK. I beg your –

MRS GARNER. A blackamoor, Mr Frank. Nothing against them. Cocks in bottles. Best place for them. Very educational. Trip down memory lane, Mr Frank. Oh yes.

She starts, as if she's seen a ghost.

FRANK. What?

MRS GARNER. Oh I rather think I recognise this one... though of course it's difficult to know in this light and after quite so many years –

FRANK. Shh. Shh. It's that sound again. Can't you hear – ?

MRS GARNER. No. Actually I can only hear my heart pounding against whalebone. Can we please not go? You've done your best, it was very noble of you.

FRANK. Shh. There it is again. Can't you hear that? There's this sound… and this… smell.

MRS GARNER. Well, there would be, Mr Frank, there would be, wouldn't there.

He lifts an opening glass case reverentially onto a table: it contains an entire leg and foot, dressed, and in a buckled shoe – rather like the leg of a broken doll.

FRANK. It's here. It's all right, Mrs G – I think it's embalmed. Stuffed even. But that's his shoe – all those years in want of a leg and here it is – dressed for Act Five. (*Reads.*) 'The leg of the illustrious Mr Foote, lost in a bet, comedian at the Haymarket, the modern Aristophanes. Full amputation performed by Mr Hunter in one and a half minutes. Anatomical lecture by appointment.'

MRS GARNER. Oh, that's disgusting. Oh no. I can't bear to look at it.

FRANK. We had an agreement. We will bring it to Westminster Abbey, to Poets' Corner, for burial along with the rest of him. And we will take it there, Mrs Garner, under your skirts.

MRS GARNER. Angels and ministers of grace defend me – we will do no such thing.

FRANK. It's not as if it would be the first actor up there.

MRS GARNER. Huh!

FRANK. We'll call it bodysnatching.

MRS GARNER. How dare you! Even stage management draws a line somewhere. Up my skirts? Up my skirt?! I am not a squeamish woman, I think you know that, I work with actors – but I am not walking across Piccadilly with a dead man's stiffy up my personal linens.

Unseen by her and FRANK, JOHN HUNTER *has entered.*
Scottish surgeon and anatomist. He is wearing a dissecting
apron and a surgical cap over his hair. He is heavily blood
splattered and carries a blunderbuss. Their backs are to him
such that he does not immediately recognise them.

HUNTER. I can give you ten seconds to explain yourselves
before I call the watch. Or I can save us all the pother and
shoot you right now for trespass.

MRS GARNER (*smuggling the leg under the apron at the front*
of her dress). Don't shoot, Mr Hunter – it's us – we were
locked in after the late lecture. I'd curtsy, sir, only, only I am
a sufferer of the gout as you know. In fact, I was hoping, if I
saw you tonight, I might ask you, I know you must get this
all the time, and I know you are less about the general
medicine than the… surgical… but about my gout –

HUNTER. Frank?

FRANK. Mr Garrick is arranging for the funeral, sir.

MRS GARNER (*edging towards the chandelier rope with her*
'third' leg)….hugger-mugger.

HUNTER. Well well. Did you know, Frank, there is no law of
trespass against the body? Nobody owns a corpse. Least of
all the corpse.

FRANK. Sir?

HUNTER. This is a theatre of science and of reason, Frank, and
if damnation existed I'd be damned if I hand over a single
curio that funds my work here, and the *lives*, the real lives,
sir, not your spirit ones – and the *real lives* that it saves. Your
plan was to put your master back together so he can dance a
jig with the quick and the dead? Well, God's bollocks to that,
sir; this is a theatre of medicine. So, madam, you'll forgive
me if I observe that you appear to have, for a woman of your
age and occupation, one more leg than is considered
medically apposite.

MRS GARNER. Ah.

FRANK. He doesn't belong to you, sir – he didn't want to be pitied – sir –

HUNTER (*aiming towards the window*). If I shoot the Watch will come –

MRS GARNER. Then shoot if you must but spare the gin bottle –

MRS GARNER *lunges forward towards the chandelier rope. Bang! – the sound of a blunderbuss being misfired and breaking glass.* HUNTER *is thrown backwards, and at the same moment the chandelier crashes to the stage floor, plunging the scene into semi-darkness again.*

Leg it!

Scene Two

Drury Lane. The wings. Twenty years earlier.

CHARLES MACKLIN *is performing as Shylock in* The Merchant of Venice, *Act Three, Scene Two, opposite* HALLAM *as Antonio.* MACKLIN *carries a cane as Shylock.*

MACKLIN/SHYLOCK.
        'Gaoler, look to him: tell not me of mercy;
        This is the fool that lent out money gratis:
        Gaoler, look to him…'

MRS GARNER (*appearing much younger, now moving nimbly, with sheaves of paper, directing things in the wings, motioning the way for* YOUNG HUNTER *and* PEG). This way, young sir. Shh. They can hear you out front. Mind the ropes. And the pisspot – the actors use it. You can't. You can sit here.

HUNTER (*also younger – his surgeon's cap removed to reveal long red hair tied at the back. He speaks in his original thick*

Scots accent). Thank ee, missus, here's payment fo' y' troubles, as weel and f' his.

He hands over a coin that she pockets.

MRS GARNER. Indeed. And if you sit here, young miss. I know you know the theatre, but this isn't your roustabout Dublin Smock Alley, this is your Theatre bloody Royal, Drury Lane, missy, and don't you fuckin' forget it.

PEG (*thick Dublin*). Ah, drop dead, y'arsy trollop.

MRS GARNER. Water off a duck, Miss Woffington, water off a fucking duck – you pays your money you sit here and learn yer King's English. You'll need it if you're ever going to work the boards in London. The only thing that matters here more than words, missy, is how you speak them. And yous – (*Motions the chairs lined up for the elocution lessons.*) yous all speak them like donkeys.

They watch MACKLIN *for a moment.*

He was Irish an' all – (*Signalling* MACKLIN *onstage.*) but he's learned some gentlemanly ways and the best speaking voice in your English-speaking theatre. So you mind your fuckin' manners, Miss Woffington, and maybe one day you'll have more than Irish tits to charm us with.

GARRICK (*thick Lichfield/Birmingham accent*). I'm so sorry. I'm late. Good evening. Mrs Garner, Miss Woffington.

MRS GARNER/PEG. Shh.

GARRICK. Sorry. Yes. Sorry.

HUNTER. Do we sit doon here then?

MRS GARNER. Shh – yes – the Wednesday-night wings are set aside for Mr Macklin's elocution pupils. Other nights, gentlemen pays to watch the dancing girls from here, if you get my drift. I've wiped the bench.

GARRICK (*incomprehensibly to* PEG *and* HUNTER). Have you seen just his Shylock so far?

PEG. Oi saw his Hamlet 'n' all – oi tort oid wit m'self.

GARRICK.... I'm sorry.

PEG. Oi sid oi saw his Hamlet 'n' all – oi tort oid wit m'self.

HUNTER. He pleed Edinburgh tee.

MRS GARNER. It's the tower of fucking Babel...

MACKLIN/SHYLOCK (*partly under above*).

   'I'll have no speaking: I will have my bond.'

*Exits the stage to applause and enters backstage area as
scenes continue onstage.*

Mrs Garner – a towel, my love. Thank you. Who have we
here?

MRS GARNER. Miss Woffington returns –

PEG. Oim lovin' every second of it so oi am, Mr Mack–

MACKLIN. I 'am'. 'Am.' Like ham. And I should know. Not
'oim' like –

MRS GARNER (*taking money from* GARRICK). Coin?

MACKLIN. Well, that would be half a rhyme, would it not,
Mr –

MRS GARNER. Garrick.

MACKLIN. Yes, I know. Garrick, yes. From Lichfield. Yes.
How is it that the middle-lands that gave us William
Shakespeare gave us also the most egregious accent in the
English language?

GARRICK. Did they?

A very beautifully dressed woman, ELIZABETH
CHUDLEIGH, *enters and takes her place by* GARRICK *and
an empty chair. She wears a very unusual feather in her hair.*

MRS GARNER. Miss Chudleigh.

MACKLIN. Miss Chudleigh – (*To* GARRICK.) and what happened to your lumbering friend?

GARRICK. He says he'll no longer to the playhouse, well, not backstage, Mr Macklin...

MACKLIN. Pity. Like that American fellow.

MRS GARNER. Franklin.

MACKLIN. Franklin, yes, Johnson and Franklin. No sense of How to Speak. All the words in the dictionary are not worth a tinker's tuppenny on the page, it's how you speak them, Miss Chudleigh, Miss Woffington. Isn't that right?

PEG. Oim – I am – sure 'tis, Mr Macklin, sir.

MACKLIN. Very good. How long till the interval class, Mrs Garner?

MRS GARNER. I'd hazard five minutes, Mr Macklin. Mrs Bellamy's Portia takes her time.

MACKLIN. She does indeed. The quality of mercy is sometimes strained. And tell Mr Hallam I need to see him in my dressing room immediately the interval curtain's down. God's teeth but Hallam's bad tonight –

MRS GARNER. The Lord Chamberlain is in, and young Prince George –

MACKLIN. That'd explain it. Send him to my dressing room as soon as he is off.

MRS GARNER. Sir.

Enter SAM FOOTE *with both legs and an air of happy disregard that he is late. He sits on the bench.*

FOOTE. Miss Woffington, I presume? Woof.

As scenery movement, lights and ropes, and applause signal the interval – FOOTE *takes the applause as if for himself.*

(*To* PEG.) Yes, I'd heard you were joining us. Sam Foote. Probably you've heard of me.

PEG. No.

FOOTE. No? My uncle killed my other uncle, my father married my aunt, we're a close family.

PEG. Oh. That's you? Charmed.

FOOTE. Mr Garrick – here's a change to the law.

PEG. And you new to London too?

FOOTE. I am. Well, I was here twice on the long vacs from Oxford, as a student, but in debtors' prison mainly, which doesn't really count as presented-at-Court, does it? Or does it? Maybe it does. And you must be the debutante.

CHUDLEIGH *nods, says nothing to all his prompts.*

Silence is so underrated on the stage –

She mouths something.

GARRICK. Chudleigh.

FOOTE. Oh. Miss Chudleigh. Yes, I see you'll go far. Nice feather. We're wasted on the law, Mr Garrick, you and I, I thought it would be all wigs and silk stockings, but not nearly enough, not nearly enough. And who's your unnervingly ginger friend?

HUNTER. Jock Hunter, sir – from Edinburgh.

FOOTE. Heaven forfend – a Jacobite – (*Swapping to perfect impersonation of* HUNTER.) So are ye of the Bonny Prince Charlie persuasion and here to attack the British Crown, Mr – ah ye honest to God called 'Jock' Hunter? – (*Swapping back to his own.*) or are you just here to expunge that heathery accent?

HUNTER. That's 'Gentleman-Surgeon' *I-am-honest-to-God-called-Jock* Hunter. And no, I have no quarrel with the Crown, sir, in fact I am on a mission to Hanover in the near future and –

PEG. Which is why he needs to be intelligible in your strangled Hanoverian English.

FOOTE. Well met by footlights, proud Miss Woffington. Where is Franklin?

MRS GARNER. Attends Mr Handel at the Italian Opera – along with half our audience, it seems.

FOOTE. I thought it was quiet tonight. Can't compete with Handel in full oratorio. Here he comes –

Re-enter MACKLIN.

MACKLIN. Mrs Garner – are we now well met? Get Hallam out of my dressing room and into the green room where he can rehearse keeping his hands off my stage props and standing *downstage* of me. Who's this?

MRS GARNER. Samuel Foote, sir –

FOOTE. We met briefly at your lessons in Bath.

MACKLIN. Ridiculous name. Is it real?

FOOTE. Yes.

MACKLIN. Well, we have a fool, a mute and a doctor – we are ready for the *commedia dell'arte* if nothing else. Jesus. Where were we?

PEG. You asked us to learn verses, sir; *Midsummer Night's Dream.*

MACKLIN. So I did. Miss Woffington – you prepared verses?

PEG. Oi did – I did.

> 'Feed him with apricocks and dewberries
> With purple grapes, green figs and mulberries...
> And for night-tapers crop their waxen thighs
> And light them at the fiery glow-worm's eyes
> To have my love to bed and to arise –'

MACKLIN. Stop. That last line again – 'thighs', 'eyes', 'arise', Miss Woffington.

PEG (*touches her heart and gestures on 'have my love'*).
> 'And light them at the fiery glow-worm's eyes
> To have my love to bed and to arise.'

MACKLIN. Stop. What's that? (*Gesture.*)

PEG. That's '*grá-ar-leith*' 'particular love', Mr Macklin. In English they only have 'love' – Mrs Sheridan taught it to me in Dublin, and Mrs Goldsmith taught her.

MACKLIN. Did they. Carry on.

PEG. That's all I learned, so please you, sir – but I know Juliet and Calista and Polly Peachum.

MACKLIN. Thank you, no. Coming along. We'll have Mr Garrick I think – you've been at your Oberon?

GARRICK. In the manner you suggested –

MACKLIN. Indeed. We attend. And speak up – they'll be old people out there – they need to know they're not dead.

GARRICK *steps forward. His style is very natural, and rather good. His accent based on* MACKLIN*'s London-neutral.*

GARRICK.
'I know a bank where the wild thyme blows
Where oxlips and the nodding violets grows...'

FOOTE. He's very good, isn't he. You're very good.

GARRICK *plays this increasingly towards* PEG *and immitates her loving gesture.*

GARRICK.
'Quite overcanopied with lush woodbine,
With sweet musk roses and with eglantine:
There sleeps Titania, sometime of the night,
Lulled in the flowers...
And with the juice of this I'll streak her eyes...'

MACKLIN. Very good, Mr Garrick. Coming along. You're sounding very London. It is nature we seek, as in the sciences, Mr Hunter. Miss Woffington – we may not need your semaphore of love, though Mr Garrick clearly appreciated it. We have better lighting in London than your smoky Smock Alley, we should rely on the true countenance of humanity. It is the modern way. An audience sniffs a lie like a dogturd. Synaesthesia, Mr Garrick – you can make them smell by what you say, I think that's what Mr Shakespeare is getting at here; colours are harmonies, voices are silk – one sense transfers to another, in the theatre. Mr Foote.

FOOTE. Sir.

MACKLIN. What have you prepared for us?

FOOTE. My Bottom.

MACKLIN. Of course you have.

MRS GARNER. Five minutes, Mr Macklin.

MACKLIN. Thank you. You have four and a half minutes, Mr Foote, to charm us with your Bottom.

FOOTE. Indeed.

(*In perfect* GARRICK *Lichfield Brummy*.) 'Pyramus draws a sword to kill himself, which the ladies cannot abide.'

GARRICK. Hey!

FOOTE. 'Write me a prologue and let the prologue – '

MACKLIN. Stop. Thank you. Very amusing, Mr Foote. You have a rare gift indeed. Though of course there are parrots and mynah birds who do the same. Don't rely on mimickry to make an audience believe in you, Mr Foote – eventually they despise a buffoon. Jokes are like Coram bastards, no one knows who begat them and when they die no one mourns – did you prepare verse as well?

FOOTE. I did.

MACKLIN. Which character?

FOOTE. Titania.

MACKLIN. The Queen of the Faeries?

MRS GARNER. Mr Macklin.

The second half is beginning onstage.

MACKLIN. Quite. This is the age of surfaces, Mr Foote, but not for Mr Shakespeare – he shows us the backstage and wings, the fullness of humanity. Which is why he is the writer, Mr Garrick, Mr Hunter, for the science of acting, the natural mind of man, not bombast, not just the joke. Mr Foote – your Faerie Queen will have to wait. I am summoned by the call of Thespis – or at least by Mr Hallam's haranguing of his audience.

Exit MACKLIN *to the stage area where his performance is greeted by applause,* The Merchant of Venice, *second half beginning Act Four, Scene One, continues, half in view.* MISS CHUDLEIGH *gets up as if to go.*

HUNTER. One second, vain glorious fool, the next – Shylock...

MRS GARNER. Miss Chudleigh, I had you down just for the interval class, yes? – I feel sure Mr Macklin can attend you in the morning for private elocution.

HUNTER/GARRICK/FOOTE. Miss Chudleigh.

Exit MISS CHUDLEIGH.

PEG. Well, thank feck for that, sure I thought she'd never shut up.

Their attention returns to MACKLIN, *who strides off angrily and grabs his Shylock hat.*

MACKLIN. Where's my fucking cane?

MRS GARNER. Mr Hallam took it, sir.

MACKLIN. Is this a theatre or visiting time at Bedlam?!

MACKLIN *returns to the stage – something is awry.*

FOOTE. Shh – gentlemen – the science of acting –

Or is it? Something is much awry in the courtroom scene – there is a fight breaking out, the elocution class move in order to see better what is going on. There is a piercing scream.

MRS GARNER (*running across the stage*). BRING DOWN
    THE CURTAIN! QUICK! – water. And wine. And a cloth.

PEG. What's happened?

MRS GARNER. Bring down the curtain! – go and tell the
    orchestra to play something. Anything. Handel. Is there a
    doctor in the –

PEG. There is.

HUNTER. I'm a surgeon not a doctor, I –

> MACKLIN *enters carrying* HALLAM, *covered in blood,
> hand clasped to his eye.* MACKLIN *wails in the manner of a
> grand tragedian.*

MACKLIN. Alack alack!

GARRICK. What's happened?

MRS GARNER. Mr Hallam has been stabbed in the eye.

MACKLIN. Oh woe.

FOOTE. With what?

GARRICK. But the swords are nibbed.

MRS GARNER. Not with a sword, you nidget. He was stabbed
    with the walking cane.

HUNTER. Through the eye?

FOOTE. That's a somewhat overplayed gesture, wouldn't you
    say?

MACKLIN. What have I wrought? What have I done? I was
    wanting to gesture at his eye, not spear it through – ohh.

PEG. Jesus, Mary and Joseph, did the Lord Chamberlain see?

MACKLIN. See? SEE? Hallam was centre stage exactly
    WHERE I SHOULD HAVE BEEN. Of course the Lord
    Chamberlain saw – so did half of London.

FOOTE. Well, I wouldn't say half, most are at the Handel –

HUNTER. Set him here. Mrs Garner, get some towels and sit him upright – you can't tourniquet for a head injury. Where's the pisspot?

GARRICK. What?

HUNTER. The pisspot – Mrs Garner said there was a pisspot.

FOOTE. Can you not wait, man?

HUNTER. Not for me. It's for the eye. The treatment for eye injuries is urine.

GARRICK. You cannot be serious.

PEG. You put piss on eye wounds?

HUNTER. Hippocrates and Fallopius both agree – every surgeon knows – it's how they treated Harold at Hastings.

FOOTE. Well, that fills us with confidence. It's empty.

HUNTER. In Edinburgh we only used the urine of maids.

GARRICK. What?

PEG. Don't look at me.

MACKLIN. Miss Woffington, if he dies it'll be murder, with six hundred witnesses including the Lord Chamberlain. Might you not try?

PEG. I don't think I could.

FOOTE. I will. I never liked him.

FOOTE *starts unbuttoning.*

MACKLIN. Has it come to this? Has it come to this?? Is this what I have wrought? This, this to be his final exit? A cane through his brain and pissed on by an overdressed molly?

FOOTE. I am not overdressed.

PEG. I'll do it. Give me the pot. Jaisus.

MRS GARNER. We've brought down the curtain, Mr Macklin – what would you have me do? Shall I send on the dancers? Or are we carrying on without Mr Hallam?

MACKLIN. All may yet be well – if he rallies it will bring the house down –

PEG. I'm trying, I'm really trying here –

HUNTER. Don't. Miss Woffington. It's too late.

GARRICK. Oh God.

MRS GARNER. Empty the house! Empty the house!

MACKLIN. May flights of angels sing him to his rest.

PEG. He's dead –

MACKLIN. It's over.

FOOTE. Well.

That's not funny.

Scene Three

The Bedford Coffee House.

MRS GARNER *is at a sort of 'bar', reduced to serving coffee to* GARRICK *and* FOOTE. *Enter* HUNTER, *in a long travelling cloak.*

HUNTER. I can't stay – I sail for Hanover on the midnight tide. Is there news from the trial?

MRS GARNER. Mr Macklin is to be branded.

FOOTE. He is acquitted of murder, but to be branded.

GARRICK. Not the face.

MRS GARNER. No, not the face. He's been banned from the stage. Can't even teach. I'm reduced to this, and he'll be destitute –

FOOTE. Says he's going to write his memoirs. Says he's going to call it *A Word in your Eye*.

GARRICK. Look, Hunter; that's why we asked you here.
The Lord Chamberlain needed an excuse for the Censorship
Act, and now he has it. Macklin proved it – we are rogues
and vagabonds.

HUNTER. We?

FOOTE. Actors.

HUNTER. Oh.

MRS GARNER. Rogues and vagabonds.

GARRICK. Safe from arrest at a Theatre Royal only.

FOOTE. No political comedies. No satires.

GARRICK. No mention of religion of America or Scotland,
naturally. All new plays to be submitted to the Lord
Chamberlain's censors. Everything.

FOOTE. So you see, we've got a scheme to put to you –

Enter PEG *in hooded cloak.*

PEG. Two feckin' ales – no make that three – what are yous
having? Oh and a pipe and some tobaccy, Mrs G. I'm late. I
know. 'Just one more song, Miss Woffington.' 'Will you sit
on my lap, Miss Woffington?' I played Desde-fucking-mona
in Dublin and it's come to this: titty-ditties for old pricks in
London clubs, so much for the land of Shakespeare. I'm
sorry – Jock – lads –

FOOTE. Rough crowd, Peg?

PEG. No longer. I'm here. And the night's still young. And
here's my favourite boys.

GARRICK. And we wanted to explain our plan, Jock.

FOOTE. Our little circumvention of this Theatre Act.

PEG. I need a London debut.

FOOTE. We need a launch, as it were, a way to start, 'Gentlemen
– and a Lady – never yet seen upon the London stage.'

GARRICK. We want to take Macklin's ideas; nature, not artifice.

PEG. Reality and youth.

FOOTE. Maybe some character roles.

GARRICK. The Theatres Royal are a closed shop. But the Little Theatre on the Haymarket.

HUNTER. The Italian opera?

MRS GARNER. The flea-ridden little music hall opposite –

PEG. – has a summer season slot –

HUNTER. But you can't do plays there.

GARRICK. We can't put a *new* play on, it isn't free yet anyway – it's got a concert season.

FOOTE. So we've thought of a plan. We need a temporary stage and –

PEG. Shakespeare. Nobody does him any more except the Irish.

GARRICK. He suits our style. You see Shakespeare, he has the inner and the outer man, as Macklin said, it's like your new light, on the mind –

FOOTE. – and the occasional clown – we were thinking, 'Young Gentlemen, never yet seen upon the London Stage.'

GARRICK. 'And the celebrated Miss Woffington.'

PEG. 'Visiting from Dublin.'

FOOTE. 'And the celebrated Miss Woffington.' That way you see we are not 'professionals' and need not submit to the Lord Chamberlain for a licence. If we play Shakespeare.

PEG. And if we charge for tea.

HUNTER. What?

FOOTE. We charge for the tea, not the play.

PEG. It was Ben Franklin's idea – we are calling it a Tea Party.

GARRICK. And playing Shakespeare. *Richard III.*

FOOTE. With some comic songs of mine for the late crowd…
maybe in a dress –

GARRICK. – maybe.

PEG. And billing ourselves as amateurs –

HUNTER. Do people want to see amateurs?

PEG. They want to see themselves. Let the crowd discover us –
vote with their tea –

GARRICK. Acting by the people.

FOOTE. For the people.

PEG. With real people in it.

GARRICK. Just more beautiful –

FOOTE. – or funnier.

PEG. Please.

HUNTER. Sounds… very modern. Enterprising. I am a great
admirer – of you all. I just don't see where I –

PEG. Surgeons' Hall, in Lincoln's Inn Fields –

FOOTE. – your Anatomy Theatre.

GARRICK. Practically the West End –

HUNTER. Oh. No –

Scene Four

Back of the curtain call, Surgeons' Hall.

The sound of ecstatic applause. The curtain call of Richard III.

MRS GARNER *is holding a curtain, ready to open it, drinking surgical gin, and counting for the benefit of* HUNTER.

MRS GARNER (*opens the curtains to look*). Seventy, seventy-one, seventy-two – oh – slight dip – oh no they're off – seventy-five, seventy-six –

PEG (*dressed as Lady Anne – but in Georgian style, a mere nod to Tudor fashion or headgear and her own shift dress*). Oh, Mrs G – have you ever heard anything like it?! I think they could carry on all night.

MRS GARNER. Here's hoping they won't.

Enter GARRICK *as Richard III, with hump, he straightens, laughs, kisses* PEG *passionately and then heads back onstage for more applause.*

PEG. Did you ever?

MRS GARNER. I did not – you get back on there, Miss Woffington – it's your night too. Again.

FOOTE (*in Shakespearean hat as Buckingham*). Did you ever?

PEG. Never – Dublin was never like this. I think the smell of blood here maybe helps!

FOOTE. No it's you. And your Davy. You go back on –

She goes – more wild applause.

MRS GARNER. It's good of you. To give them their time. It's very fleeting, as I recall. In fact – it's only really good before you've even begun. Love and theatre. It's good of you to take me on –

FOOTE. Mrs G – we'll have seasons making hay now – the Shakespeareans and the clown.

GARRICK *re-enters again briefly.*

GARRICK. Come on, Sammy –

MRS GARNER. I think you should go on. Go. Go on.

Wild applause, cheering. MRS GARNER *is left on her own, raising a gin to them and downing it and taking her own curtsy.*

Scene Five

FOOTE*'s Haymarket dressing room.*

The passing of time and the growing success of our three actors is signalled perhaps by the descent of a series of lavish character costumes... Handel music and the reveal of the relatively grand Haymarket dressing room featuring twin dressing tables. Over the course of the play, this dressing room becomes yet more elegant – and eventually features an adjoining bedroom.

FOOTE *is changing out of eighteenth-century men's clothes, and putting on make-up. Slowly he changes into the undergarments and corset of a Georgian lady – this is not apparent until halfway through this scene.*

MRS GARNER (*wears a chatelaines waistband with many keys and a fob watch*). I'm glad you're in – it's already the half, Mr Foote, for the afterpiece – because I need to talk to you about Mrs Clive's dresses, they need letting out again, and Mr Barry. He is complaining about his dressing room again, Mr Foote – I found him measuring it and he is right, Mr Foote, it is smaller than Mr Jewell's, and you know how Mr Barry is about Mr Jewell –

FOOTE. And good evening to you, Mrs Garner.

MRS GARNER. Good evening. And this invitation to Mr
Hunter's lecture series – (*Handing him an opened letter.*) oh,
and I've been through all the new billing too, and Mr Jewell
wants to talk to you about that too, and Mr Barry wants to
know if Mr Garrick has asked Miss Woffington about that
thing she does in Act Three.

FOOTE. That thing?

MRS GARNER. That thing.

FOOTE. Oh, that thing. Have you asked Mr Garrick?

MRS GARNER. Mr Barry asked me to ask you to ask him to
ask her.

FOOTE. I see. And is Desdemona dead yet?

MRS GARNER. Indeed she is, sir, she's waiting to do her song
and watching Mr Garrick from the wings, I believe.

FOOTE. Is she now. How's the house?

MRS GARNER. Fair to middling. Mr Handel is playing, sir…
But Mr Garrick and Miss Woffington do seem to have won
them over now with the strangling of Desdemona. I think
plenty will stay on for your afterpiece, sir.

FOOTE. After two hours of Davy's pauses they'll be in need…

MRS GARNER. There's as many as come to see you as to see
him, Mr Foote. And the Prince may come late, sir; there's a
reception at the Palace.

FOOTE. Mrs G.

MRS GARNER. Sir?

FOOTE. Nothing… Actually. I was wondering, do you know,
Miss Woffington seemed… not quite herself last night. Is
there any…

MRS GARNER. You mean does she have Lady M visiting?

FOOTE. What? Yes. No! I mean. I wondered if she had heard the news of Mr Garrick's... engagements.

MRS GARNER. His engagement at Drury Lane, sir, or the other one?

FOOTE. Both.

MRS GARNER. I believe she has, Mr Foote, I dare to say she has. Because I saw her sticking hatpins into a rag doll yesterday and she sent out for extra make-up, so yes, on the whole, I'd say she'd heard.

FOOTE. Thank you, Mrs G... oh, I thought I'd wear the yellow tafetta for the second afterpiece this evening. And, Mrs G – any response to the advertisement?

He begins to don a lady's wig and mob cap.

MRS GARNER. None as were suitable. Two illiterate country lads, one with half a thumb, which is hardly ideal in a dresser, sir.

FOOTE. I see.

MRS GARNER. It's never easy to find respectable servants for the theatre, sir – that, and I think... (*Looks* FOOTE *up and down, who is now dressed in women's petticoats*.) what with the troubles in America...

FOOTE. Yes, never mind. We will struggle on – oh, and, Mrs G.

MRS GARNER. Yes, sir – I'm actually needed in the –

FOOTE. Yes, of course. Go – go on.

FOOTE *is already in wig, corset and petticoats. There is a knock at the door.*

Enter.

Enter FRANK, *a young Black man.*

FRANK. Begging your pardon, miss, am I too late?

FOOTE *is about to say something but changes his mind, and plays along in higher voice.*

FOOTE. That rather depends. For Mr Garrick's Moor, you
could probably still catch that tetchy business with Iago, but
as for Foote's Molly Midnight, you are still early for the late
show. Come in.

FRANK. Oh. May I wait for Mr Foote here, miss? I was told he
was here, but maybe he's watching Mr Garrick like everyone
else, miss?

FOOTE. I see. You're not from London, are you?

FRANK. I am as English as you are, miss, I am a freed man
since I stepped ashore.

FOOTE. Yes, well legally that rather depends, look, there's
something I should explain –

FRANK. I was baptised this morning, miss, St Margaret's,
Westminster. So they can never send me back – I'm a free
Briton and His Majesty's loyal subject.

FOOTE. Absolutely – I mean you don't seem... au fait with the
ways of the theatre –

FRANK. No?

FOOTE. No.

FRANK. I need work, miss. I've been a houseboy and a
footman. My young master died at sea, miss. They said if I
escorted him across the oceans I would be granted my
freedom in England. I learn fast. I collect words.

FOOTE. Is that so? Storm tossed.

FRANK. Here's my character – (*Handing over a letter.*)

FOOTE. I see. If you're in service in the theatre, you'll never
get a respectable position again, you know that? (*Reading.*)
Jamaica? You're a free man now – you should aim higher.

FRANK. Actually... there is a sort of theatre there, miss, in
Kingstown, the young master took me – he needed carrying
that is. And I read and write, miss, and... I've read a play.

FOOTE. Oh? Which one?

FRANK. *Othello.*

FOOTE. What did you think?

FRANK. I thought it was very funny.

FOOTE. Well, that's certainly not the received view, but it's mine too as it goes – much ado about a handkerchief.

FRANK. I beg your pardon, miss?

FOOTE. Look, there's something I should tell you you may find a little shocking – I was thinking you might like to sit down, Mr –

FRANK. Frank.

FOOTE. Mr Frank – do you have a surname?

FRANK. My owner's name was Bathurst, miss, but I had myself christened Barber, miss – I am Mr Frank Barber.

FOOTE. Well, Mr Barber, if you can take what I am about to tell you like a free Briton, which is to say, with a love of the ridiculous and a disinclination to sneer, then I shall be offering you the job for which you came – I am not 'miss'.

A pause as it sinks in.

FRANK. Not?

FOOTE. Miss. My name is Samuel Foote. Mr.

FRANK (*after a pause*). I can take that… like a free Englishman.

FOOTE. Good. When can you start?

FRANK. Tomorrow. Tonight. I – thank you, sir –

Sound of wild applause, off – GARRICK*'s curtain call.*

FOOTE. Your duties are that of a footman and a valet plus a little that you would not have done in the Indies; namely, line learning with me, and lacing me in. Oh, and another thing – this dressing room I share with Miss Woffington some

nights. She is sometimes here, sometimes at Covent Garden.
She's singing on a swing at the moment. Anything you see
happen here you must consider a play-act only. And nothing
that happens in a theatre dressing room is ever discussed in
what they call the real world. I hope I make myself clear.
You'll be on the company split, but I shall tip you every
Benefit Night, monthly. There. Do you have any questions?

FRANK. No. Yes. Do I have to wear a – [dress]?

FOOTE. You do not. You *may*. It has been known. Indeed there
has been wide suspicion about Mrs Clive this many-a-year,
but no, you should dress as you are.

MRS GARNER (*re-enters backwards with* FOOTE*'s costume –
the fancy outer bit*). Oh, sweet heavens.

FOOTE. This is Mr Frank Barber. From the West Indies, but
now of our Little Theatre on the Haymarket. Mr Barber, this
is Mrs Garner, the prompter. She is in charge. Of everything.

Would you be so good as to show him where the play rolls
are kept.

MRS GARNER. Very good. Come with me, young man...

As they are leaving, GARRICK *enters, as Othello.*

GARRICK. Well, Sam, I think we can safely say I have them
eating out of my blackened hand for you and – oh –

MRS GARNER. Begging your pardon, sir, we was just leaving.

FOOTE. Mr Barber, the Moor of Venice, Mr Garrick, the Moor
of Kingston.

GARRICK. Your new dresser?

FOOTE. The same.

GARRICK. Well well. Excellent choice. We might use you for
the Court of Cleopatra next week – do you act? No. Stop.
Don't say a word. Better the silent noble savage. I'd have
you in *Othello* but I fear it might show up the deficiencies in

my make-up. Reality on stage tends to overwhelm the acting
– this is one of the salient mysteries of our art.

FRANK. Sir?

FOOTE. Mr Barber was just going to be shown the ropes, Davy
– I'll be down by midnight, Frank, so I shall see you then –
there's food in the wings usually. Be careful not to eat
anything belonging to Mrs Clive. She can't bend over any
more, but she can bite.

FRANK. Really?

FOOTE. No. Look, actually, if you like, sit out front and see the
afterpiece –

FRANK. Truly? The theatre? May I – ?

FOOTE. You may. You are a free Englishman, that is what it is
meant to mean.

FRANK. Thank you, miss. Thank you, sir.

MRS GARNER *and* FRANK *exit.*

GARRICK. Sammy, how long have we known each other?

FOOTE. Since the Plantagenets – I don't know – I'm on in a
few minutes and –

GARRICK. What do you think of me?

FOOTE. Of you? Of the celebrated Mr Garrick? The world's
foremost exponent of the pause?

GARRICK. As a man.

FOOTE. Oh, as a man. You're asking me?

GARRICK. I think you know me as well as anyone. If you had
to say. In a court of law.

FOOTE. Are you in trouble?

He passes GARRICK *a bowl of water and a towel for his
make-up, which he helps remove.*

My friend Mr Garrick is chiefly remarkable for his eyes and
his well-turned leg, his love of life, his narcissism... mind
you, he's the best company in London and a man who knows
more about the workings of the human soul than any cleric I
know – and I know a few... you just don't know much about
yourself, Davy. What do you want me to say? Mr Garrick is
an actor. He is the opposite of a man.

GARRICK. Oh.

FOOTE. Peg has her quick change in a moment.

GARRICK. I've been offered Drury Lane. A season of
Shakespeare.

FOOTE. I know.

GARRICK. Oh. And the money to take a company to Stratford.

FOOTE. Where?

GARRICK. Warwickshire. It's where the Bard was born.

FOOTE. Do they know?

GARRICK. In Warwickshire? – God no – illiterate oiks, but the
new mayor thinks we can put on a – 'Jubilee Festival', raise
funds for his town hall.

FOOTE. Well, that's a ridiculous idea. No. You can't do this.
You can't. You'd ruin us here, you know that. We have only
the summer seasons to try to recoup... and we need
Shakespeare to evade the censors. Look; it's very impressive,
Davy, it really is, the Shakespeare statue, your Shakespeare
lectures. But we will never be respectable, you and me.
We're actors.

GARRICK. My parents came to see *Hamlet* again last week.
My father's dying you know. Properly this time. Very
convincing. And he said to me 'When are you going to settle
down, Davy?' and I tried telling him that, you know, we take
eight hundred pound a season here, and that's rather more
than in the wine trade or the law, but unreliable I know,

unreliable, and, as you say, not respectable, not the sort of
thing they can tell their friends back in Lichfield and, he
said, 'I just don't see, David, how you're ever going to make
a fist of it.' Me.

FOOTE. We never get the genus of love we want, Davy –

GARRICK. So I told him I was going to marry.

FOOTE. Who?

GARRICK. Does it matter?

FOOTE. Probably to whomever you asked. Have you told
Peg?... I see. So you're not taking her to Drury Lane and
Stretford.

GARRICK. Stratford.

FOOTE. Stratford.

GARRICK. The intended Mrs Garrick does not approve.

FOOTE. No woman approves of Peg. Every man does. It is the
secret of her singular allure. Pass me my fan. I think you
should tell them. Both.

GARRICK. Yes. Yes I do see that. Though of course then
nobody will love me. And I'd thought you'd need Peg here.

FOOTE. I do.

GARRICK. What?

FOOTE. Need Peg. End of our happy menage, then. Yes, well
then – sod tragedy; comedy's conspiracy of silence. I know –
we'll use puppets, they can't censor puppets, we'll call it
Punch and Judy... I think she does know. I think she had
been waiting for you to mention it. I assume, ideally, when
you are not fucking her.

FOOTE *is now in full drag and ready to head on.*

Was that it, then? I hope this man-to-man has been helpful.

GARRICK. I am not a bad person, Sam.

FOOTE. Of course not, Davy. You're a weak one.

MRS GARNER *pops her head around a corner.*

MRS GARNER. Beginners for the afterpiece, Mr Foote.

PEG *is entering as* FOOTE *is leaving.*

FOOTE. Thank you, Mrs G. Oh, Peg darling, when you come on later – as the Milkmaid of Human Kindness – I was thinking, that thing you did with your pails last night – very funny.

PEG. Davy.

She signals that GARRICK *still has make-up on, and spits and cleans it off, like a mum – while onstage* FOOTE *makes his entrance as Molly Midnight, so the scene runs straight into Scene Six.*

Scene Six

FOOTE*'s afterpiece: 'Mother Midnight' runs concurrently upstage with the scene back in the dressing room.*

FOOTE *onstage.*

FOOTE.
'To please at once the gallery, box and pit
Requires at least, no common share of wit,
So spare a thought for those who tread these boards
Who 'personate great queens but shift with lords.'

PEG (*her accent now rather actressy at times, less so when talking to* GARRICK, *he is helping her change*). Do you know what Sam said to me the other day – could you help me with this? – we always pass in the scene dock in the late-night Molière parody – and he whispered, 'Would you fuck me for three shillings and better billing?', and I said, 'Feck off,

you're as queer as a coot and I'm as famous as the Queen of
fucking Sheba,' and he said, 'Well then, would you palm me
off for a thousand guineas?', and I said, 'Jesus, Sammy, is
there nothing happening for you over in St James's Park these
days, sure I'd fuck the Pope for a thousand guineas'. And he
said, 'Well then, how about a fiver to screw Prince George,
we could do with a Theatre Royal licence', and I said, 'You
rotten old pimp; screw him yourself! Offering out my
services! What do you take me for??' And he said, 'Well, I
think we've already established that, so let's start haggling!'
Let's start haggling! You've got to give it to him. So I
punched him in the face but he went on anyway.

GARRICK. I love you.

PEG. I swear Mr Barry's Cassio takes longer every night. It's not
even his Benefit, when I'd, you know, give him the benefit.
He's just so slow. We've added ten minutes since last season.
I'm having a – can you pull this, thank you – I'm having a
word with Mrs Garner about Othello's pillow as well – I dread
to think what the dancing girls are using it for, but it smells
like a badger's scrotum and that's not the thought Desdemona
needs when she's dying for mispriz'd love.

GARRICK. I said I love you.

PEG. Yes, I heard you, Davy. You say it all the time. Pass me
that bottle, will you?

GARRICK. I love you.

PEG. You say it at the footlights and you say it to the Ladies of
the Court who want to con their Shakespeare and you say it
to the feckin' bootboys for all I know and you say it to me
every time... you've said it to me a lot, Davy.

GARRICK. I don't know what I want, Peg.

PEG. Oh you poor... fuckdoodle, Davy. Look, Davy – go to
Drury Lane. Do your Shakespeare Jubilee, sure the good
people of Buckfuck-Whereshire will be thrilled and we'll all
still be waiting for your Lear and then maybes we can all get
over yourself. We'll be fine here. Sammy'll write more

comedies, I'm back doing Calista in *The Fair Penitent* next week, always pays the bills, and we'll find a way to run ahead of the censors, I'll find some lord with an annuity and a weak heart...

GARRICK. I'm not a young man any more, Peg.

PEG. No.

GARRICK. I'm nearly thirty-four. They've asked me to play Lear. I have to think to the future. I'm sorry.

PEG. Yes.

GARRICK. Peg. I've been wanting to ask for some time.

PEG. Yes.

GARRICK. Because I know you watch, and you notice these things.

PEG. What, Davy?

GARRICK. Peg, do you think, from the back of the gallery, they can see my hair is thinning?

PEG. Davy – I – I think... you and me... I think I'm just not very good at the farewell scenes. I used to quite like you as Romeo, once you were dead.

GARRICK. I think I am just about to do the thing I will regret most all my life.

PEG. Then don't do it, Davy.

Onstage.

FOOTE.

'How hard, how hard is the Condition of our Sex?
Through every State of Life the Slaves of Men?
Shake off this vile Obedience they exact,
And claim an equal Empire o'er the World!...'

Back in the dressing room.

FOOTE *enters.*

GARRICK. I was just –

FOOTE. Pausing?

PEG. Leaving. Mr Garrick was just making his exit. Maybe sees you later at The Bedford.

GARRICK. Yes. Maybe.

Exit GARRICK. *Silence.*

PEG. Do you know what I saw Mrs Clive doing in the shifting room yesterday?

FOOTE. Eating I'm imagining?

PEG. Making up her hands. The backs of her hands. She said she could fool anyone she was thirty, in the right light, if she could just hide the veins on the back of her hands... I imagine Davy's taking Susannah Cibber as his Desdemona and she'll do Juliet I'm imagining. She's very good. And her Lady Anne. Perhaps a little arch, in my opinion, as Calista.

FOOTE *kisses her forehead or they make some shared gesture of complicity, in silence.*

Scene Seven

Royal Society Lecture rehearsal at Hunter's Operating Theatre.

Electric sparks fly.

The scene moves, as with the actors, from 'rehearsal' into actual lecture.

BENJAMIN FRANKLIN *is standing by his Leyden machine (electric batteries); it crackles with static.*

HUNTER. Electric fluid. The Leibniz lecture series continues with a discourse between Mr Benjamin Franklin, from the Philadelphia Assembly –

FRANKLIN. And Mr John Hunter of the London Company of Surgeons. Royal Company?

HUNTER. *Royal* College is our plan. A discourse we have titled: The Theatre of the Mind. Am I still sounding too Scottish?

FRANKLIN. I'm hardly the man to ask, Mr Hunter.

HUNTER. Mr Franklin will be familiar to many of you from the air-pump experiments last year and the new St Bride's lightning conductor, as indeed for the opinions he has expressed about his native Pennsylvania. Do you want me to say that?

FRANKLIN. No. No. No politics. 'The purpose of our Leyden jar is to demonstrate three items. One: the existence of "electric fluid" – familiar to us all as static, the spark we feel on greeting a winter stranger. We believe, after Bishop Berkeley, that this is the same fluid that gives language to existence. Two: "electric fluid" can be stored, like milk but – Three: like milk will curdle – deteriorate – though fresh electric fluid can be generated as if from the udders of the universe.' This is where we can extinguish more candles, Mr Hunter, the better for you to see Peg Woffington's eyes light up – '

HUNTER. 'The purpose of the discussion and our experiment is this: electric fluid can be directed, like a lightning bolt, like a sentence.'

FRANKLIN *causes a spark to arc across between two bottles.*

Our discourse further represents electric fluid as one of the two languages, if you will, being spoken in the brain.

FRANKLIN. One being electric.

HUNTER. And the other the coursing of our blood.

FRANKLIN. She'll like that.

HUNTER. Mr Franklin, you mistake me. My interest in the theatre is academic. And *Mrs* Woffington's affections are... contracted.

The lecture for real.

Our thesis is that the mind works with both electricity *and* the blood but in the manner of a Great Theatre in action; pulsed messages that are then rehearsed into meaning. And that can be stopped by a blockage.

FRANKLIN. The brain as known to us from this anatomy theatre differs from Count von Leibniz's concept of a 'mind' just as an actor, who can function as a mere conner of lines –

HUNTER. – differs from an actor who can breathe the electricity of laughter into meaning, into... a Theatre of the Mind.

More sparks fly.

Scene Eight

The Haymarket dressing room.

FRANK *and* MRS GARNER *are polishing shoes and combing and setting wigs.*

MRS GARNER. Cues and lines. Cues and lines. Each roll a part. A role. You see. Altogether, it makes up a play. Only the audience gets the full meaning. And Mr Foote likes his things laid out on the table, so. It's a blood sport, Mr Frank, and we're the gamekeepers. Oh, and you have to empty the pisspot.

FRANK. And why in dresses?

MRS GARNER. There's no explaining that. It's all part of growing up and being British, Mr Frank. I dare says you have your funny ways in Jamaica.

FRANK. Sugar and raping slaves you mean?

MRS GARNER. Well – no – I –

FRANK. I was wondering… I was wondering if there was a Mrs Foote.

MRS GARNER. Mr Frank. You're a dark horse, aren't you?

FRANK. So they tell me.

MRS GARNER. Well, it may disappoint you to learn that there was, in point of fact. Young actress. Sweet thing. Married him in debtor's prison before he was famous, but saw the error of her ways. Or his. But we don't mind that in the theatre, do we –

FRANK. And a Mr Woffington?

MRS GARNER. Ha! Well, you'd have to pity him if there were. No. Miss Woffington has graduated to the married state as a matter of billing, Mr Frank, and to allow her gentlemen callers to know they need not singly keep her.

FRANK. Oh.

MRS GARNER. So if you see her hat on the dressing-room door, you'll know she has a Friend of the Haymarket Theatre visiting.

FRANK. I see.

MRS GARNER. Who Sponsors the Arts.

FRANK. Yes, I see.

MRS GARNER. No, the point is you don't see, Frank. Ever.

Enter FOOTE.

FRANK. Good evening, sir.

FOOTE. Frank.

FRANK. Shall I get more coffee?

FOOTE. God, no. I'm already shaking like the Lisbon earthquake. Is Mrs Woffington in yet?

FRANK. She is not. We are running out of wig powder, sir, shall I get more from the baker's?

FOOTE. Yes, do. Charge it to my account.

FRANK. Yes, sir. *The Maid of Bath* tonight? (*Holding up a dress.*)

FOOTE. *The Maid of Bath*. Did she say she would be late?

FRANK. Not exactly, sir… She left with Lord Sandwich, sir, and some others. I think they were going to the Beefsteak Club. She said she might not be at the dance rehearsals today.

FOOTE. And was she?

FRANK. I believe not.

Enter PEG, *opening a letter.* FOOTE *begins to change into Lady Coldstream from* The Maid of Bath (*Scottish Dowager*).

PEG. Jesus, Frank, thank Christ you're here – would you run to the coffee house for me. I'll take a pot-full of their blackest, and Mrs Wight's head compress from the 'pothecaries on Panton Street – would you be a dear?

FOOTE. So it was a night, then?

PEG. It was.

FOOTE. You know the Prince is in tonight? I'm starting with one of the Tea Party sketches, the one about George Washington and the Stamp Act, and then it's the *Maid of Bath*.

PEG. Right-oh. It's billed as a tea party, then?

FOOTE. Of course – and then it's a puppet interlude, and then if the Prince stays, I'll do The Auctioneer late-night, you can join in if you're up to it, and if he goes, Molly Midnight or Lady Pentweazle, for old times' sake.

PEG. Excellent. I'll be fine, Sam – (*Having opened another letter.*) What do you think – should I sit for Reynolds or for Zoffany? I can't decide. Both want me, but only if the other doesn't. What do you think?

FOOTE. I'd go with Reynolds – good with eyes and tits. How was your… afterpiece.

PEG. Well, it went rather well since you ask. Sandwich is an admirer. Luckily he's a gambler too. A girl has to think to the future.

FOOTE. Indeed. He seemed very taken with your britches scenes.

PEG. He said he was so taken with all five acts, he would run to five acts himself.

FOOTE. Ha! An idle boast – I hope you took the bet.

PEG. So I did – and the rest of the table at the Beefsteak bet too.

FOOTE. And could he?

PEG. Now a lady wouldn't tell, Sam. So… Well, of course I thought he couldn't – he'd been drinking since the vote in the Lords at three… but yes, actually. Five acts. Quite impressive. A rather laboured finale…

FOOTE. Well, I hope you paid up.

PEG. Certainly not. What do you take me for? Like I said, he's a gambling man – I told him: double or quits!

FOOTE. Ha! Garrick's playing Lear tonight.

PEG. So I hear –

FOOTE. And Handel is rattling the box-office coffers as well. I'm surprised the Prince is coming.

PEG. Well, he's not a fan of *Lear* – hardly a model of kingship. Look, Sammy, I am going to have to ask: can we carry on like this? My last Benefit Night, I felt like I'd slept with half the audience, and it still didn't net me even fifty guineas – do we not need a play, a proper play. Could we not put some tragedy back on the menu? I don't just do tits and teeth, you know.

FOOTE. I know.

PEG. I was thinking, we've done all your Molière translations, how about something more *tragedie-française*, something grand, in Alexandrines, with a throne, Sammy, and lots and lots of incest... and then we can do the comedy afterpieces... after.

Re-enter FRANK *with coffee pot, wig, etc., and letter.*

FRANK. Your coffee, Mrs Woffington, and your compress. I've recurled your wig for Molly Midnight, Mr Foote, and a message for you from front of house.

FOOTE. Thank you, Frank.

PEG. Frank, could you be a sweetheart and tell Mrs Garner that Lord Sandwich will be here during Mr Foote's afterpieces to discuss the Haymarket season.

FRANK. Of course, Mrs Woffington.

FOOTE. Peg – you may want to be putting your dress back on.

PEG. Not *The Maid of Bath*?

FOOTE. Not yet – Hunter says the Prince wants to visit – they arrived early and he's already in the royal box and clearly insufficiently amused.

PEG. Does he want to discuss the Haymarket season?

FOOTE. Of course not. Behave yourself.

Enter MRS GARNER.

MRS GARNER. Oh, sweet Lord – Frank – quick, hide the pisspot behind that screen and find a wig – there's one stage left where the cat sleeps – knock out the fleas and put it on.

FRANK. The cat?

MRS GARNER. The wig, and do up your waistcoat and look exotic. Mrs W – shall I lace you in?

PEG. I am fine, Mrs Garner, we've met before, the Prince and I – and his brother, and indeed two of his uncles. Who were particular admirers of the Irish arts.

MRS GARNER. Oh, sweet heavens.

HUNTER (*off*). This way, Your Royal Highness –

PRINCE GEORGE (*off*). He doesn't mind being interrupted – (*Entering*.)

Enter PRINCE GEORGE *and* HUNTER.

FOOTE. He does not, Your Royal Highness. I am but the servant of my audience always.

PRINCE GEORGE. Quite so, quite so. Yes. One went to see Mr Reynolds last week at work in his studios just here in Leicester Fields. The arts-in-progress. Fascinating. Yes. Ain't it odd; but people must tell you this all the time – you look so much smaller in real life...

HUNTER. May I present Mrs Woffington.

PRINCE GEORGE. Oh, we've met. I fell in love with Mrs Woffington's Titania.

PEG. When I was a miss.

PRINCE GEORGE. And my brother and I saw your Juliet in Dublin – 'That I were a glove upon that hand, that I might touch that cheek.'

PEG. Your Royal Highness should have been my Montague.

PRINCE GEORGE. Not really, I was ten.

FOOTE. We have a new comedy for you tonight, my own fair hand – a gentle play on the manners of Bath, gallants at the pump rooms, ladies in disguise as footmen...

PRINCE GEORGE. Well well, good good. Bath. Good clean fun.

FOOTE. Nothing as might offend your mother, Your Royal Highness, or your gracious grandfather.

PRINCE GEORGE. Quite. That's somewhat what I came to speak of, Foote. We are charged with lightening the load of my grandsire's days at Windsor, he is not well, and my brother and I have been arranging musical evenings.

FOOTE. Aha.

PRINCE GEORGE. Handel, mainly.

FOOTE. Aha.

PRINCE GEORGE. But my brother the Duke of York and I, we hit upon the idea of something more –

FOOTE. Fun?

PRINCE GEORGE. Theatrical.

FOOTE. Theatrical.

PRINCE GEORGE. And English. Something more for an English King. At Windsor. So we hit upon the idea, which is what I am getting at here, we hit upon the idea of some Shakespeare.

PEG. Oh?

PRINCE GEORGE. At Windsor, at Whitsuntide. And Garrick thought of you.

FOOTE. Did he?

PRINCE GEORGE. That you – and Mrs Woffington, might oblige us by joining Mr Garrick and some of the Theatre Royal Company.

FOOTE. An honour for us mere comedians I'm sure – *The Merry Wives* I am assuming?

PRINCE GEORGE. Well, yes and no. Garrick has rewritten –

FOOTE. Of course he has.

PRINCE GEORGE. Some of those Henrys he's been doing at...

FOOTE. Stretford?

PEG. Stratford.

PRINCE GEORGE. Stratford. Yes! Lots of kings. And Princess Katherine of course – (*Signalling* PEG.) some of the choicest bits of Windsor with Falstaff.

FOOTE. Aha.

PRINCE GEORGE. And Garrick as old King Henry. And I was thinking of Mistress Quickly. (*Signalling* FOOTE *in his dress.*)

FOOTE. Oh, I see.

PEG. Does Mr Garrick not want to play Hal? – he was very good as Hal?

PRINCE GEORGE. Ah, well therein hangs a thing… we thought, to please my grandfather…

FOOTE. Oh, oh, I see – but of course, 'A gentlemen never yet seen upon the stage.' I see – a royal command performance. You are a prince amongst players, sir. At your service.

PRINCE GEORGE. Very good. That's settled then. Mr Garrick says we can meet here to 'rehearse'. A little Harry in the night. What what. 'Once more into the breeches.' Good. Come, Mr Hunter. Let us go and admire art from afar. *The Maid of Bath*. Excellent. I imagine you play some roaring girl disguised as a page?

PEG. I imagine so, Your Royal Highness.

PRINCE GEORGE. What is it they say, Mr Foote? Break a leg?

FOOTE. I believe they do.

He bows. Exit PRINCE GEORGE. HUNTER *goes to follow* – HUNTER *handing* FOOTE *another letter as he goes – the National Anthem is starting.*

HUNTER. Another invitation for you. The Royal Society. And The Bedford later if HRH heads home? Mrs Woffington.

Exit HUNTER.

FOOTE. Well, we might be broke, but we are the Prince's Men – powdered wigs, decorum and drop the knob gags – what say you to that, Mrs Woffington?

PEG. Fuck me – Windsor!

FOOTE. As a general or a specific invitation? He's a married man, Peg.

PEG. Ah, but his wee brother so isn't.

Scene Nine

Hunter's Anatomy Lecture Theatre – another animated lecture.

HUNTER. 'Think of a phrase, any phrase. The first thing that came in to your head. Now. Write it down.'

That was your instruction I gave you as you first sat here. Thank you for your cooperation. Our experiment is known as a 'Panjandrum'. One of you only was asked to write a phrase with the word 'panjandrum' in it. The rest wrote non-sense – or it became nonsense, non sequiturs, when strung together by our secretary.

FRANKLIN *hands him a piece of paper.*

Thank you, Mr Franklin. A panjandrum devised by you, the Royal Society. My question is this. How do actors learn their lines? Thousands of them, hundreds of new scenes every season. Can the brain be worked like a Leyden machine, new routes of electric fluid established, ideas stored. Do we have our guest, Mr Franklin?

FOOTE *is guided on by* FRANKLIN. FOOTE *is sporting both earplugs and a blindfold.* FRANKLIN *hands him the paper and temporarily undoes his blindfold while* HUNTER *takes out his fob watch.*

While we reflect on the indignities heaped upon the famous, the celebrated Mr Foote will have thirty-five seconds in which to commit to memory your non-sense. Are you ready, Mr Foote? Thank you, Mr Franklin.

FRANKLIN *re-blindfolds* FOOTE.

FOOTE. Now? 'So she went into the garden to cut a cabbage leaf to make an apple pie and at the same time a great she-bear coming up the street pops its head into the shop: "What! No soap?" So he died and she very imprudently married the barber and there were present the grand Panjandrum himself with the little round button at the top and they all fell to playing the game of catch as catch can till the gunpowder ran out at the heels of their boots.'

HUNTER. Congratulations. Word perfect. What have you to say to that, Mr Foote?

FOOTE. Thank God the Royal Society isn't writing comedies.

HUNTER. Mr Foote charges his young actors to learn such within *one* reading, one reading only, unaided by sense or story.

FOOTE. May I take this off now?

HUNTER. But what is going on in the brain as this happens? 'How do you learn your lines?' It turns out it's the most important question you can ask.

FOOTE. Please may I take this off now?

FRANKLIN. The dark art that actors and rhetoricians share raises this question: in establishing rhythms that become pathways in the mind, do we have a sense of truth that may not be real?

HUNTER. So I ask you now sitting there to listen differently – to hear your mind constructing meaning, from language as Leibniz has it. As well as the image of this famous man in a theatre there is also a *sense* of you seeing him. Feel it. This presence is sedate and quiet.

FOOTE. Not in my theatre it isn't. May I take this off now?

FRANKLIN. This half-known presence may be your mind. Stepping into the lit stage is the movement of the free mind into an understanding of itself.

HUNTER. This is what we believe 'consciousness' means.

FRANKLIN. Might we ask you again, Mr Foote?

FOOTE. How I learn my lines?

The scene merges into the next, as FOOTE *carries on learning lines to his latest prologue, and* HUNTER *and* FRANKLIN *exit. The dressing room and* MRS GARNER *and* FRANK *appear around* FOOTE *helping him change his clothes.* MRS GARNER *has both the lines and her account book.*

'And how do you spend your days?'

– wait, I've got it –

'In pastimes, prodigality, and plays!
Where giggling girls, and powder'd fops may sit,
Or shall you all be cram'd into the pit?
And crowd my stalls for Satan's Benefit.

Scene Ten

The Haymarket dressing room.

MRS GARNER *as she checks the script.*

MRS GARNER. Nearly. 'Old Nick's Benefit' you've got here. That's three-and-six for the new costume for Mrs Clive, and the musicians are insisting on more money again – they say they have to stay later because of all the laughter – and the candlemakers are pressing for payment, lighting this place is ruining us. And the musicians…

FOOTE. If only we could do it in the dark and silently.

MRS GARNER. It's not funny, Mr Foote – we can't make it to the end of the season. These all need paying – most within the week.

FOOTE. Right. How's box office?

MRS GARNER. It has been very unseasonable weather, Mr Foote.

FOOTE. Right.

MRS GARNER. And the West End – it's in a shocking state, Mr Foote. You should see the gutters – running with piss and gin vomit. The quality don't want to face it on a Saturday night.

FOOTE. Indeed.

MRS GARNER. Piss and gin.

FOOTE. Indeed. Thank you.

FRANK. Mr Garrick is mounting another season of Shakespeare.

FOOTE. Which ones this time?

MRS GARNER. Well, all of them, actually, is his latest idea, Mr Foote – all the best bits run together. Less of the boring wordy-bits.

Enter PEG.

PEG. Afternoon – 'Here's a remarkable convenient place for our rehearsal.'

MRS GARNER. And then there's the Pleasure Gardens to compete with, Mr Foote, and of course Mr Handel has a new opera opposite.

FOOTE. Oh God – Another Handel? I offer comedy sans consequence, he offers singers sans balls.

FRANK. They don't have…?

FOOTE. They do not. They are removed by Vatican barbers –

PEG. Priests can be very enterprising…

FOOTE. I mean to say, we all believe in suffering for our art, but it's ridiculous – chop off your knacks and you'll be loved by every woman in the audience – could any joke be crueller?

PEG. When Farinelli and Urbani did their duet, people used to actually weep with the beauty of it –

FOOTE. Can you credit it? A simple two-hander, and not a dry seat in the house.

MRS GARNER. And not one bollock between them.

PEG. Yes I heard it was a two-hander.

FOOTE. What?

PEG. Farinelli's cock, a real Italian and no chance of getting caught with child – you can see the appeal.

MRS GARNER. Even before it turned out what he lacked in the sack he made up for in the shaft –

FOOTE. Desist! Please, ladies. The point is this, Frank, the musical, like the poor, is always with us. We carry on. But I'm having a word with Garrick. It has to stop. He has a Theatre Royal licence, it seems to me colonising all of Shakespeare, even the comedies, it's just unfair.

PEG. Hear, hear. Tell him we shall mount our own.

FOOTE. Ha! *Othello the Comedy* – what do you say, Frank?

FRANK. *Much Ado About a Handkerchief.*

PEG. Sam.

FOOTE. Peggy, my love.

PEG. Is John Hunter in tonight?

FOOTE. I believe so – he usually comes to a first night – why?

PEG. I owe him money is all. Sam –

FOOTE. I would if I could, Peg – you'll get money directly come your Benefit Night, but the box office is…

PEG. No I know, sorry. I shouldn't have brought it up.

FOOTE. Never mind – here comes Roscius to my Aristophanes –

Enter GARRICK, *expensively dressed.*

GARRICK. 'Well here's a wondrous convenient place' –

PEG. I've already done that one.

GARRICK. Mrs Woffington.

PEG. Mr Garrick.

GARRICK. The Prince not here yet? I see Handel's got something new on. Bloody castrati. When is he due?

FOOTE. Any moment. His equerry said he'd come incognito via Suffolk Street, disguised as my washerwoman.

PEG. Like Bonny Prince Charlie?

GARRICK. Don't mock monarchy, Peg. The theatre hangs by a small royal tassle... So, Sam, I see you've bought the house next to stage door?

FOOTE. I have.

GARRICK. Shows proper confidence in the future of your Little Theatre.

FOOTE. And less in my ability to find my way home. It's rather handy actually – I can sneak between sheets between acts. I hear you've bought a villa in Hampton.

PEG. With an *island*.

GARRICK. Oh, pish. It's just a little island.

FOOTE. And building a temple to Shakespeare on it.

PEG. With a statue of the Bard looking a lot like –

FOOTE. David Garrick.

GARRICK. Now that's not true.

PEG. We're only teasing, Davy. We all bask in your glory, and happily.

GARRICK. Hmmm. Mr Foote less happily methinks.

FRANK. Stage door says there's a funny-talking washerwoman asking for you, Mr Foote, and you as well, Mr Garrick.

FOOTE. Send him up, Frank, with or without my smalls. Mrs Garner, you have the rolls?

MRS GARNER. I do indeed, sir, my own fair hand, as copied from Mr Garrick's: *The Pleasant and Diverting Royal Historie of Kings Henry IV and V and VI* by Mr Garrick and Mr Shakespeare.

GARRICK. Hardly me at all. It just all ends happily.

Enter PRINCE GEORGE – *all stand* – *he hands a woman's cape and washing basket to* MRS GARNER.

PRINCE GEORGE. No ceremony please – 'So shaken as we are, so wan with care.'

PEG/GARRICK. Oh very good, sir!

PRINCE GEORGE. Mrs Woffington, your servant. I had to come like this to keep it all –

PEG. Tush-tush?

PRINCE GEORGE. Quite.

MRS GARNER *cackles*.

FOOTE. Might you, Mrs G, find something suitably regal for the Prince's Prince Hal in the props room?

Exit MRS GARNER.

GARRICK. I thought, sir, we should start with Act One, Scene One – Prince Hal and Falstaff?

FOOTE. Very well. In the absence of our prompt, could you read in the stage directions, Frank?

FRANK. Me, sir? Yes, sir. 'The Pleasant and Diverting – sorry – Windsor. A tavern. Enter Sir John Falstaff.'

FOOTE (*as Falstaff, with Northern Irish accent*). 'Now, Hal, what time of day is it? Hal, I prithee swet wag, when thou art King – '

GARRICK. Is he going to do it like that? Are you going to do it like that?

FOOTE. Like what?

GARRICK. Like an Ulster molly.

FOOTE. I thought it rather suited. Shakespeare doesn't say anywhere he's not.

GARRICK. But it doesn't say anywhere he is.

FOOTE. Well, I can't see how I can distinguish my Mistress Quickly and my Falstaff unless I have an accent.

PRINCE GEORGE. You'd have a dress.

GARRICK. But you can't play Quickly if you are playing Falstaff. Obviously. You can't play a scene with yourself.

FOOTE. You manage well enough.

GARRICK. Can we just get on – the Prince hasn't all day.

PRINCE GEORGE. I probably do actually –

FOOTE (*as Falstaff again, less Ulster*). Hal, I prithee, sweet wag, when thou art King, let not us that are squires of the night be called thieves of the day's beauty –

PRINCE GEORGE. Did I not say, Mr Garrick, he was the very man?

GARRICK. Indeed you did, sir.

FOOTE. Mr Garrick is unhappy if we at the Little Theatre at the Haymarket venture towards the Bard, which is his purview.

GARRICK. You have Tea Parties, satirical puppets and Mrs Woffington's comic timing – I have poetry and Shakespeare.

FOOTE. And a Theatre Royal licence.

PRINCE GEORGE. I'd wager the Little Theatre on the Haymarket could give you a run for your money, Mr Garrick, at least with Shakespeare's comedies.

PEG. Oh a bet, I like a bet.

PRINCE GEORGE. Do you gamble, Mrs Woffington?

PEG. I have been known to play double or quits, sir.

GARRICK. Tragedy versus comedy?! It's clear which one triumphs, sire, in the arts – it's hardly an even bet.

FRANK. *Othello the Comedy*?

PRINCE GEORGE. Who's this?

FOOTE. This is Mr Frank Barber, of Kingston, Jamaica, sire, and a freeman of England.

PRINCE GEORGE. Who thinks *Othello* is a comedy?

FOOTE. It is an opinion he is well-placed to voice.

PRINCE GEORGE. Well well – how's that, Garrick – *Othello the Comedy* opposite *Othello the Tragedy* – the same text – Mr Shakespeare's that is, and see with which the audience finds most affinity. Ha! How's that? In which, though, would Mrs Woffington play her Desdemona?

PEG. Oh, that's easy, sir. I've parried my Desdemona around Mr Garrick's pauses already – and I'd always take a wager with Mr Foote.

PRINCE GEORGE. What say you? Mr Foote – we could make a scientific experiment of Shakespeare! Can London not be the capital of America and the capital of theatre as well?! What what!

Re-enter MRS GARNER, *carrying prop crowns*.

MRS GARNER. There's an equerry at the stage door, Mr Foote, looking for the washerwoman as came earlier.

PRINCE GEORGE. Ugh. Tell him to send up a message if it's important. Where were we?

GARRICK. Rehearsing.

FOOTE. *Othello the Comedy*? The wager?

PRINCE GEORGE. Ah yes indeed –

MRS GARNER. He says you are to come at once, sir, please begging your pardon, sir, Your Royal Highness – but he would not come in.

GARRICK. Why ever not?

MRS GARNER. He said it would be improper.

PRINCE GEORGE. 'So wan with care' indeed. We have our exits and our entrances, and mine are not mine own. I'll see what message is so vital it attends not Mr Shakespeare – thank you, gentlemen, Mrs Woffington – I shall hope to return.

Bows and curtsies. MRS GARNER *and* PRINCE GEORGE *exit.*

GARRICK. *Othello the Comedy*?

PEG. I think it might work.

GARRICK. I absolutely forbid it, Sam. I came here to rehearse. I offer you a little royal largesse, a little respectable trip to Windsor, and what do you do? Molly Midnight as Falstaff and *Othello the Comedy* – have you nothing to say?

FOOTE. I'm pausing.

GARRICK. You will not make a laughing stock of Shakespeare – his name is all that stands between us and vagabondage. You know this. Shakespeare is what makes theatre respectable. His poetry is what makes theatre theatre – that is what Shakespeare means.

FOOTE. Pish. If Shakespeare can't take a joke, he's not an Englishman. I need to stay afloat here, Davy, and if everything else in London is open to satire I see no reason why Shakespeare shouldn't be too – God's teeth, man; your Temple to the Bard, and your bloody Stratford Jubilee. There's one word, you know, one word that only the English have – I mean, obviously, we've thousands – but one word as has no translation in any or ancient language. Do you know what it is, Davy?

GARRICK. I feel sure you are about to tell me.

FOOTE. 'Cant'.

PEG. Oh no, that translates into Gaelic.

FOOTE. Cant. Cant. Peg. Cant.

PEG. Oh.

FOOTE. Hypocritical and sanctimonious talk, or in your case, Davy, self-serving, nationalistic, bombastic claptrap. Bard my arse. I'm going to mount a Shakespeare season and I'm going to call it Garrick's Cant.

GARRICK. If you do this, this is war.

FOOTE. Then war it is. 'Respectable', Davy? Who ever gave a fuck about that – keep us just one whisker from the magistrates, that's all I ask *Othello the Comedy*. I'm in – and what's more, begging your indulgence, Mrs Woffington, I might even play Desde-fuckin'-mona.

Enter Mrs GARNER.

MRS GARNER. Gentlemen. Madam. The equerry – the message he couldn't deliver to the Prince. In a theatre. The old King. He's dead.

GARRICK. The King is dead. Long live the King.

FOOTE. Oh for God's sake, Davy, this isn't a play.

MRS GARNER. Well, I think it just turned into our tragedy – they're shutting all the theatres in mourning.

FRANK. God Save young King George!

PEG. Sure George'll be fuckin' fine, Frank – God save all of us.

Scene Eleven

Hunter's Lecture Theatre.

FRANKLIN *enters in full mourning clothes, processing carefully with something in a bell jar, covered in black. The cloth is removed to reveal a knifefish suspended in preservative fluid. There is also a very beautiful 3D model of a horse's nervous system.* FRANKLIN *practises for a moment his upcoming lecture with his props.*

FRANKLIN. Is he coming?

HUNTER. Why wouldn't he? The theatres remain shut.

FRANKLIN. 'Anatomists and philosophers and even politicians must march in step. This fish, the knifefish, communicates with electricity. Not this one obviously, being dead. As hounds inhabit a world of smell, knifefish live in electric fluid. We seek the language in which the human mind swims.' Can you not deliver this thesis? It's yours by rights.

HUNTER. It's ours. But I cannot now. You'll be fine.

Enter FOOTE, *out of breath.*

FOOTE. I'm sorry. I had to take the backstreets for fear of creditors. One more week. London awaits a coronation like a nun expecting ravishment, quivering in sackcloth – it's bankrupting me. What's this?

FRANKLIN. A knifefish.

FOOTE. Of course. So. My counsel as rhetorician. I am honoured.

FRANKLIN. Our penultimate talk for the Royal Society. It's Hunter's thesis, but now he's surgeon to a king, I think he'd rather not deliver something so radical.

HUNTER. Mr Franklin has an interest in improving his
delivery.

FOOTE. I shall play Macklin to your Demosthenes; he was a
stutterer, you know. Personally, I found dressing up in
women's clothing helped my rhetorical confidence... I'm not
suggesting it for the Royal Society – I'll heckle from the
wings, shall I?

HUNTER. Funny you should say. We've dedicated it to you.

FOOTE. To me?

FRANKLIN. We believe we are conscious of the 'out there' like
an audience looking down on a world of light. These sounds
and sights, me, this moment, you, the audience – these
messages are received, we believe, as small lightning bolts
of electricity in your brain.

FOOTE. Very good. Legs apart. Eyes front. Dedicated to me? –
Sorry, chin up.

FRANKLIN. But messages come like call boys at the theatre;
late. What we cannot work out is how your brain produces
its play and you, your consciousness, centre stage, rounded
with a sleep. But we suspect the past is talking to us. What
you recreate in your mind has happened already. Mrs
Woffington has sung. Mr Garrick and Mr Foote have left the
stage, but the call boys are still ferrying messages to your
brain. It is already over.

Scene Twelve

Backstage at the Haymarket.

FRANK *has entered with two black wigs, and* MRS GARNER *is preparing for an opening night; a tray of glasses, costumes. The sound of an orchestra.*

FOOTE. What's that infernal noise?

PEG. It's Handel, Sam – the windows are all open at His Majesty's, it's a hot night –

FOOTE. – is all we fucking need our first night back.

> FRANK *begins to black him up as Othello during this scene.*

MRS GARNER. The candlemakers are at the stage door now the theatre's reopening, what do you want me to say?

FOOTE. Oh God – tell them – tell them I will pay them mid-season.

MRS GARNER. I already tried that, sir, they say there's candles for opening night and that's that until you pay up.

FOOTE. Right. Perfect.

FRANK. It always works out, Mr Foote – that's the lesson of every play seems to me – it always works out. The occasional implausible coincidence and accidental incestuous relationship, but by and by it all turns out well. More black, I was thinking.

> FRANK *exits.*

FOOTE (*to Mrs GARNER*). How do I look? – we'll be doing the play in the dark soon enough anyway; the tight curl I think – (*Replacing one Othello wig with another.*) is there any news from the Palace?

MRS GARNER (*exiting*). Nothing from the Palace, no.

FOOTE. Right. His bloody idea. A little royal presence would've helped.

PEG. We have friends in, Sam: Hunter, Reynolds, Franklin. The Court is still in mourning, Sam.

FOOTE. He goes to the fucking opera.

PEG. Yes, well, that's the trouble with kingship, ain't it – no more roister-doister –

GARRICK *arrives, angry. He is also blacked up and dressed as Othello.*

Oh.

GARRICK. So.

FOOTE. So.

GARRICK. So.

FOOTE. So – what, Davy?

GARRICK. So it's true then. It's come to this.

MRS GARNER *re-entering – sees them, and exits.*

MRS GARNER. Dear God! Frank!

GARRICK. Well. What do you have to say for yourself?

FOOTE. It was a royal command wager, the theatres are reopening, how could I refuse?

GARRICK. I'm on in forty-five minutes. At Drury Lane –

FOOTE. Yes, and we're on in thirty, so.

FRANK *re-enters with more wigs and make-up,* MRS GARNER *follows.*

FRANK. Sweet Jesus.

FOOTE. Yes, well – here we are for you, Frank, brothers in arms – a brace of Moors. I don't see the problem. Is there a problem? Do you see the problem, Frank?

FRANK. Erm.

FOOTE. You see, Frank doesn't see the problem. I dare say it feels just like home.

PEG. Boys, boys – look, this can be worked out. Much as this is every Desdemona's dream – I think we just need to acknowledge that London is big enough, Davy, for Sam to give his... alternative Othello.

GARRICK. Alternative? The Moorish general as rendered by a loon-faced moll with a noted penchant for lace?

FOOTE. It's a joke, Davy; that's the joke – Othello's practically commedia already; it's Venice for fuck's sake, Davy, I NEED THE MONEY.

GARRICK. You have no right to go on, as me, as Othello, tonight. Especially not tonight, when I am opening *my* Othello –

FOOTE. You you you – it's all about you – maybe mine's just a generic Othello – it's not necessarily your Othello...

GARRICK. Everyone says you've been practising my –

FOOTE. Pause? Pish, Peg was saying just the other day that I am very much my own Othello, the likes of which has never before been seen upon the London stage.

PEG. Well, I did say that, yes.

GARRICK. I'LL NOT HAVE IT, SAM. Shakespeare cannot be a joke; he was an actor too, dragging himself out of the mire – why won't you see it –

He starts pulling off FOOTE*'s wig – a fight breaks out.*

You cannot and WILL NOT – Peg, please, can you not – 'my Desdemona'.

FOOTE. 'My Desdemona' – (*In imitation of* GARRICK*'s Olivier-style Jamaican.*) it's not even proper Jamaican, Frank, is it?

FOOTE *pulls off* GARRICK*'s wig,* FRANK *tries to pull them apart, and has his hair grabbed by* GARRICK.

FRANK. Ow.

FOOTE. It's real, you fool.

GARRICK. What?

GARRICK *pulls his stage sword, only for* FOOTE *to do the same, but it's a 'girls" fight – furious and inept, they run over the daybed,* GARRICK *trips up* FOOTE *and is on top of him, with* FRANK *trying to separate them, when* KING GEORGE *enters, in riding boots, long coat and recognisable George III uniform, and powdered wig.*

PEG *and* MRS GARNER *curtsy deeply. The boys stop, and hand back each other's wigs.*

KING GEORGE. I appear to be interrupting a prize fight – Mrs Woffington, Mr Garrick? Mr Foote? I presume.

MRS GARNER/GARRICK/PEG/FRANK/FOOTE. Your Majesty.

KING GEORGE. I was just on my way to the opera but I appear to be interrupting some… convocation of blackamoors. What is the collective noun?

FOOTE. Sir?

KING GEORGE. For negroes?

FOOTE. Frank?

FRANK. I believe it is 'an injustice', sir. A coffle of slaves. An injustice of Black men.

KING GEORGE. Well well. You're the boy from the Indies, aren't you?

FRANK. Your Majesty.

KING GEORGE. Still reading?

FRANK. Yes, sir.

KING GEORGE. Good. Well well. I am sorry I cannot support the evening, Foote, or indeed yours, Garrick. I am sure you understand. Maybe next season. Once the world has... moved on. Heavy is the head – [that wears a crown]

FOOTE. Mrs Woffington and I would be honoured, always, by your presence, Your Majesty.

KING GEORGE. Yes. I only came to say – it was a shame, about Windsor.

GARRICK. Your Hal, sir? Yes, sir – you would have proved most royal, sir, had it been put on.

KING GEORGE. Thank you. How might we help here? One thinks sometimes, when one has been obliged to listen at length to the Archbishop of Canterbury, one thinks sometimes, 'What would Solomon do?' Perhaps an alternative wager? something a little more English. One just rode in from Windsor, we have a Barbary horse outside.

GARRICK. Like Othello.

KING GEORGE. Quite. How about that? I'll not need it again tonight. A time trial like Newmarket. Win the hand of Desdemona the *English* way.

PEG. Oh, this is good.

GARRICK. We are actors, sire, not jockeys.

KING GEORGE. An actorly contest then...

FOOTE. I'll wager you I can gallop round both Theatres Royal faster than you can, and still be back at the Haymarket for my first entrance.

GARRICK. What?

PEG. Oh, this is grand!

FOOTE. Against your entire month's candle budget for Drury Lane, the cost of our enlightenment, Mrs Garner. I'll go first – royal witness. The Battle of the Othellos – the papers'll love it –

PEG. And everyone wins.

KING GEORGE. Apart from, possibly, my horse. Well, that's
settled then. Fifty guineas in from me too – royalty should
sponsor the arts. Excellent. Good day to all then – let me
know who wins. Send a note to Mr Handel – it might enliven
our evening at the opera...

Exit KING GEORGE *to bows and curtsies.*

GARRICK. SAM! – good God – what has taken possession –

FOOTE. As my uncle said on the gallows, 'How could things
possibly get worse.' Fuck it. Ride a cock horse. Mrs Garner –
try to get a message to the *Westminster Gazette*, we can get a
mention in the early editions. Wish me luck.

MRS GARNER. May the best Moor win.

FRANK. Are you sure, Mr Foote?

GARRICK. This is ridiculous. This is the sort of thing that gets
us a bad name, Sam.

FOOTE. Well, God's bollocks to that. Mrs Garner – I shall be
back in ten minutes, peradventure fifteen, slightly glowing, as
befits the Moor of Venice, and expect a glass of porter, Frank,
before my first entrance. Desdemona – see you on stage –

Exit FOOTE.

GARRICK. This is insanity.

MRS GARNER. Well, I'm going to watch from the shifting
room – are you coming, Frank? – I'd wager a shilling on
Mr Garrick...

Exit MRS GARNER *and* FRANK.

GARRICK. Oh God. I'm on in about thirty-five minutes.

PEG. It takes five minutes to Drury Lane, faster on a horse. I
seem to remember there was plenty you could get done in
the half. One for the road, Davy, as we wait? Or a drink?

Sound of rearing horse, shouting. 'The King's Horse!'
'LOOK OUT!' A piercing scream. A horse rearing.

Continuation of same scene, interposed with HUNTER*'s*
'anatomy lecture'.

MRS GARNER *runs on to centre stage.*

MRS GARNER. PLEASE!!! THIS ISN'T A JOKE – THIS
ISN'T IN THE PLAY. IS THERE A DOCTOR IN THE
HOUSE? IS THERE A DOCTOR? Is there? Please. DR
HUNTER. Dr Hunter! PLEASE!

Light on HUNTER.

HUNTER. If it seems unreal, it's not. When someone cries
out –

MRS GARNER. 'Is there a doctor in the house?'

HUNTER. The world stops. A hush descends upon a theatre
when those words are spoken, a communal clenching of
buttocks for which Dr Johnson provides no word. In case it's
real. But this time it was.

MRS GARNER (*to* HUNTER). Oh thank God – quickly –
FRANK!

FRANKLIN. When I saw Hunter climbing up from the stalls, I
knew it was bad, so I followed. Foote was being half-carried
by Frank in from the stage door – concussed and bleeding –

HUNTER. Mrs Garner, fetch a strong chair. Frank, send to
Jermyn Street immediately for my instruments. I think we
should empty the house, do you not?

MRS GARNER *hauls on a stage throne.*

FOOTE. That rather depends on the sight-lines really – if we
can get centre stage –

HUNTER. This is no time to joke, Mr Foote.

FOOTE. I can think of none better – arghhhh.

MRS GARNER. Clear the house! The show is over. Clear the house. Frank – tell the orchestra to play. Anything. Loudly. Handel.

She hands HUNTER *her apron and scissors and exits. Perhaps we see her partly on the gantry, running, operating ropes.*

GARRICK. Raw white bones broke the surface of Foote's skin.

FRANK. Mr Foote's own bones – above and below the knee.

HUNTER. It is what surgeons call a floating knee injury. As Mrs Garner brought the curtain down and cleared the house I explained to Mr Foote what was bound to happen. 'Injuries like yours are almost always fatal. You must prepare yourself for the worst.'

GARRICK. Which was not, however, death.

HUNTER. I can save your life. But what I must do is simple and necessary and immediate. I must amputate your leg.

FOOTE. Oh God – oh God – Peg, where's Peg?

PEG. I'm here.

HUNTER. Fetch turpentine and water and stage ropes.

FOOTE. Peg, There's only one thing I ask if you can do it.

PEG. Anything. Anything.

FOOTE. Can you put a stop to that fucking Handel.

The Handel music gently builds through the narration of the amputation.

GARRICK. An amputee had never been seen upon the London stage. Foote knew if he lived that he would never work again.

FOOTE. NOOOOOOO!

Re-enter FRANK *with* STAGE HANDS, *carrying turpentine and ropes.*

FRANK. Speed was the most surprising of Mr Hunter's skills. Barely had the curtain been drawn but he was roping down Mr Foote into the throne.

FRANKLIN. Foote was cut from his stockings and turpentine poured over his bleeding wounds.

FRANK. Should I fetch an opiate?

FRANKLIN. But Hunter said no.

HUNTER. 'They risk diluting the patient's blood or draining the mind of its determination.'

FRANK. And I began to shake.

Enter MRS GARNER *with small table and medical bag.*

MRS GARNER. From Jermyn Street.

She hands FRANK HUNTER*'s medical bag.*

HUNTER. Scalpel.

MRS GARNER. Yes.

HUNTER. Curved blade.

MRS GARNER. Yes.

HUNTER. Saw.

MRS GARNER. Yes.

HUNTER. *Calvatia gigantea*... dried puff ball.

FRANK. Puff ball?

FRANKLIN. For a man of science; the finest theatre available in London. And Mr Foote a patient of astonishing bravery and surprising... rhetorical flourish.

FOOTE. Sweet buggering Jesus Christ on the cross.

PEG. I was asked to leave, but would not.

HUNTER. Are we ready? It is now that Hippocrates requires of me the following, Mr Foote – Sam – I ask your permission and your forgiveness for what I am about to do.

PEG. And Sammy remarked in response that of his legs, it had never been his favourite one.

FRANK. And then it began.

HUNTER. The skin of the entire thigh must be cut around the knee and from knee to groin, and ripped upwards and sideways as quickly and as firmly as possible.

FRANKLIN. Frank and Garrick had secured the tourniquet as high as they might.

HUNTER. Then I cut into the muscles halfway up to the groin.

GARRICK. At this point Foote fainted.

FRANKLIN. But was reawakened.

PEG. 'Hail Mary, full of Grace... (*Her prayers continue underneath.*)

HUNTER. The patient must not fall into coma – we believe that it kills. Next is the deep cleaving of muscle to create two sides of the stump. Pull here, Mrs Garner. Two hefts of muscle are pulled to the side and held.

GARRICK. There was a lot of blood. More than in the blinding of Gloucester.

HUNTER. One must saw gently at the beginning, until the saw is well entered, and then go on faster with discretion deep and fast into the bone.

GARRICK. More than in the murder of Duncan...

FRANK. There was a lot of blood.

FRANKLIN. Mr Barber appears to be about to faint, and Mrs Woffington does, but only briefly.

FRANK. And then, less than two minutes after the operation had begun, and less than half an hour after the accident that necessitated it, Mr Foote's leg, that I had dressed and tended so many times, drops to one side, and hits the boards like a stage weight.

The Handel music stops.

FRANKLIN. Mrs Garner brings old petticoats and heaps them up around the throne to soak the blood…

PEG.…now and at the hour of our death, Amen'.

I had somehow thought that would be all. I would be there, with towels and water and tending his brow. I have played that scene. But not yet.

FRANK. But the operation continued.

HUNTER. I expose an artery and separate the vein and the nerve that runs alongside it. Two items kill the amputee: loss of blood, or the unbearable pain of untied nerves.

FRANKLIN. Which continue in a perpetual agony of cutting if they are not tied properly.

HUNTER. So I knot and tie and knot and tie. The pulsation of the blood thumps with such force –

GARRICK. – that you could see it and you could hear it –

HUNTER. – such force that I fashion other ties as far up as I need to prevent rupture. And eventually the pounding subsides, and the nerves are tied, and a mixture of lint and wig powder can be used.

PEG. And he sewed up poor Sam's thigh like a lamb at Eastertide.

MRS GARNER. Like poorly-sewn britches.

GARRICK. And we dressed his wounds –

PEG. – and sprinkled between layers of bandages, the lint and the wig flour –

HUNTER. – and the dried *calvatia* –

FRANK. – 'puff ball' –

FRANKLIN. – which coagulates blood.

PEG. And Mr Hunter took the leg, and the stage hands took the ropes, and Mrs Garner set about the mopping of the Haymarket stage of poor Sammy's blood.

FRANK. And we carried him to his house next door.

GARRICK. With the tenderness of a mother.

FRANK. And I lay him in his bed, expecting him to die.

GARRICK. As did we all.

PEG. But he did not. And do you know what? Do you know what was the first thing Sam said, when he came out of his delirium? Do you know?

He said, he said, 'It's – '

FOOTE. 'It's going to be bloody difficult to top that in the second act.'

End of Act One.

ACT TWO

Scene One

Vauxhall Pleasure Gardens.

FOOTE *is in a bath chair. His stump clearly visible.* FRANK *wheels the chair, and holds a large parasol for them* PEG *and* FOOTE. *They are at a concert at Vauxhall Pleasure Gardens. Handel.*

FOOTE. For free?

PEG. Yes.

FOOTE. Completely free?

PEG. Yes.

FOOTE. So anyone can just – ? A free concert? Handel so fucking rich he can just compose for the sheer joy of it? So anyone can just turn up and listen?

PEG. Apart from you, clearly.

FOOTE. Do you like it, Frank?

FRANK. I preferred his earlier work.

FOOTE. Exactly. Adam Smith. If you give it away, no one really cares. I'd have thought you of all people would recognise the principle, Mrs Woffington.

PEG. We are being seen, Sam. We are being perceived. You, and my new hat. That and the gossip. Do you remember that chit of a girl at Macklin's classes? The one who wouldn't speak.

FOOTE. No.

PEG. Married the Duke of Kingston.

FOOTE. Nope.

PEG. Now come on, Sam: old goat, young maid, clandestine marriage, harlot's progress? –

FOOTE. Chudleigh.

PEG. Chudleigh. The Duke's died and now she's richer than the Virginia plantations. I tell you, I'm in the wrong profession.

FOOTE. You're in the wrong bit of the same profession.

The music comes to a temporary end. Polite applause.

PEG. Oh look, there's the King, Sammy – I think he saw you – I think he might come over. Do you think if you leaned on Frank you could stand? Do you think you could, because I think then everyone would see and –

FOOTE. I'm not an exhibit, Mrs Woffington, nor an object of pity for the adoring crowd of Mr Handel or indeed of George-the-Turd – arghhh.

FOOTE *in real pain.*

PEG. People are staring, Sam, try not to.

FOOTE. Do you know Mr Locke, Peg?

PEG. Is he a Friend of the Haymarket Theatre?

FOOTE. I doubt it. John Locke. 'Human Understanding': the existence of things proved by our ability to sense them – so what to make of a leg that burns in hellfire and isn't even there?

PEG. Your leg?

FOOTE. Arghhh. Frank – do you have the opiates Jock Hunter gave you?

FRANK. There are no more for today, sir.

FOOTE. My head.

PEG. Now your head?

FOOTE. Take me away. And this incessant Handel –

PEG. The music stopped, Sammy. Look, it's Davy – he's coming over – we can't go now –

GARRICK *enters*.

GARRICK. Mrs Woffington, Sam – dear fellow. So good to see you. So brave. Handel's on good form, isn't he? I had heard you might show yourself. Your bravery shames us all.

FOOTE. I am not a hero, Davy – I have lost a leg, it's not the same thing.

GARRICK. It looks like it to all of us, Sam. London can speak of little else, but your… retirement – such a loss to the theatre – for us all. We will lobby the King for a pension – something at Windsor, maybe, a cottage. It's a tragedy, Sam. Truly. They pay to see us be our best selves – not – (*Signals the stump.*) You must not want to be seen – of course you don't. So brave. I was wondering if I might take Mrs Woffington from you a while? A tour of the gardens? Lord Sandwich was just saying how well you are looking, Peg. And there is the new statue of Mr Handel – have you seen it?

PEG. Sam, do you object?

FOOTE. To the statue of Handel? – yes I fu–

PEG. I think a tour of the gardens would be most appreciated, Mr Garrick. I don't imagine Mr Foote has anything further to add to our duologue. Have you, Sam?

FOOTE. Exeunt. Omnes.

They go. The Handel starts up again – more plangent.

FRANK. When I first came to London, it was like stepping into a play. Piccadilly. Westminster Bridge. Things I had read about with the young master. Inebriated is the word, isn't it? The lights and the laughter. On that first night, after you gave me the job, Mr Foote, I walked back through St James's

Park, and I could hear laughter. There was a full moon. And just by the bushes, by the Queen's House, I saw these bodies, grey flesh under an English moon. And I went over. I'd never seen white people doing that, together, and laughing, in a city. Though I'd seen, you know… But where I am from, there was never laughter, because it was either quietly, back under the kitchen where we did live. Or angry. My mother fighting off the old master… and then crying. Quietly. Or the young master and me… quietly. So. It was funny, to hear laughter, in the city.

FOOTE. Well… You go into the bushes now, Frank, you'll hear them – men and their moxies –

FRANK. Oh, it wasn't women, men and women, in St James's Park that night, sir – it was two guardsmen a-buggering…

FOOTE. Of course. Queen's Own?

FRANK. Liberty. I thought. This is what it means. And I had met the sort of person I didn't know could be and I thought, when I met you, that you were free. And brave. For what you do and who you are. But you're not. You were just born with everything. And now you have slightly less.

Scene Two

Haymarket backstage/onstage.

The dressing room is as it always was, except there is now a bed. MRS GARNER *enters with rolls of paper.* PEG *is reading one, sitting on a rumpled bed.*

PEG. Is this his? He sleeps here?

MRS GARNER. He asked Frank to move it round

PEG. And Davy's coming too?

MRS GARNER. Drury Lane sent a message... but the Lord Chamberlain won't allow –

FOOTE (*off*). I come I come! See how I come!

FRANK. Easy does it, Mr Foote.

> FOOTE *emerges walking with a crutch and* FRANK*'s aid, his leg now strapped up. Both he and, later,* GARRICK *are given hats as Romeo and Tybalt by* MRS GARNER *and* FRANK *during the course of their rehearsal.* PEG *plays Juliet in her Georgian dress, perhaps with a circle of flowers in her hair.*

FOOTE. I am not an old woman, Frank, I am a footless Foote. Peg! So you like it? Is Davy here yet?

MRS GARNER. Mr Garrick's on his way, sir...

PEG. Sit down here.

FOOTE. Oh no – the show must hop on.

> *Enter* GARRICK.

GARRICK. Here. Dear fellow.

FOOTE. No sympathy. I won't have it. Pity is for the opera. There will be soldiers in the audience, for fuck's sake; I lost a leg in a bet and my name is Foote. I don't think we can ask for anything but laughter –

GARRICK. You're determined to show yourself – not even warn the Lord Chamberlain? It's never been done –

PEG. Sam, are you sure?

FOOTE. Never surer. Comedy, I was telling Frank, is all about pain. And we two should know. So, here's how it begins. Do you have your lengths?

GARRICK. So this is the first sketch? And I'm playing me-as-Tybalt? Right. Are you sure you are up to this?

FOOTE. Yes yes. You stand there. I'll enter stage left. I can't move far, so none of your upstaging.

GARRICK. Stage left. Right. This is quite short, yes, because I'll have to get back each night to Drury Lane. Where are you going to be, Peg?

PEG. On a balcony I'd imagine? Do you want to lean on Frank, Sam?

FOOTE. Peg – the stage is yours.

PEG (*reading*). 'Alack, Mr Garrick, have a heart if not a head, we owe him this.'

GARRICK (*reading*). 'Mrs Woffington, how can we allow him back on the public stage – let alone Shakespeare's? It offends – it embarrasses – and more than that, I so fear putting my foot in it. I mean, I do think it's right we help him find his feet – we'd be going out on a limb – '

FOOTE. Halloo.

GARRICK. 'Heavens, here he comes – '

FOOTE (*reads – though he knows the lines*). 'What hey – here I am, at last returned and at your bidding, Mr Garrick.'

GARRICK. 'Let me give you a hand, Foote.' This is very good. (*Flicking ahead in his script.*) Sorry. 'For the Apothecary I take it?'

FOOTE. 'Oh no, sir, I am here for the role of Master Montague.'

GARRICK. 'You wish to play the juvenile, Foote?'

FOOTE. 'Yes.'

PEG/GARRICK. 'Romeo?'

FOOTE. 'Indeed, Mr Garrick. The lovesick youth, the slayer of Tybalt, the wooer of Juliet, yes, sir. I may be a foot shorter than I used to be, but I am not the lesser lover for being lame. I am very good at fencing, sir; fully armed.'

GARRICK. Should I pause here, do you think? It's just I think they'll be so shocked – I think I'll take a pause – do you think this needs a pause, Peg? Do you want me to rehearse the pause, Sam?

FOOTE. No.

GARRICK. Right. No… it's just I think they'll – … no. Right. 'But, Mr Foote – '

FOOTE. 'A lover may be lame, Mr Garrick, the act of love requires many things but symmetry is not one of them.'

PEG. You can't say that.

FOOTE. 'I suppose Juliet might lend me a hand.'

MRS GARNER/FRANK. You definitely can't say that.

GARRICK. 'Mr Foote, I feel you are going round in circles here.'

FOOTE. 'Mind you, if I lose my other leg, I'll just be arsing around all night' – of *course* I won't say that –

Continues onstage.

GARRICK. 'So your suggestion, Mrs Woffington, for Foote's Benefit Night is my version of *Romeo and Juliet*?'

PEG. 'Audiences prefer it to Mr Shakespeare's.'

FOOTE. 'And I too am partial to its happy ending – well, I am partial to most things now.'

GARRICK. But with me as Tybalt and Mr Foote – sans foot – as Romeo?'

FOOTE. 'Is there a problem?'

GARRICK. 'No.'

FOOTE. 'Is it my age?'

GARRICK. 'No. I – '

FOOTE. 'I will here confess I am not in the first flush of manhood nor standing at the very hard, as they say, of the yard arm, but then, frankly, and if I may be so ungallant, Mrs Woffington is full three times the age of Juliet, and, Mr Garrick sir, you first played Tybalt with your own hair.'

PEG. 'Sir!'

GARRICK. 'It is not that, Mr Foote. Let me too expound – I have indeed striven many years towards the glory of the stage, and my love of The Bard of Avon is uncontested, so I have to acknowledge that your pairing with Mrs Woffington's celebrated Juliet does indeed throw up the question… of the balcony scene.'

FOOTE. 'Are you saying that I'm fat?'

GARRICK. 'No! Indeed I had been thinking you seem to have lost some weight. Oh, I'm so sorry.'

FOOTE. 'Do you feel I'm missing something, Mrs Woffington?'

PEG. 'What do you feel?'

FOOTE. 'Not enough really.'

GARRICK. 'I'm just a-feared – '

FOOTE. 'That I'll flop?… so you think I should I put my feet up? Or, on the other hand, I need a push in the right direction? For the sake of every wounded soldier present I will declare: I am more than a bit hacked-off, Mr Garrick, in fact, sir, I'm stumped.'

Laughter and applause. Change of lights to back in dressing room.

PEG. There were people weeping, Sammy, weeping.

GARRICK. In a good way.

PEG. In a good way.

Enter in haste MRS GARNER, *carrying a cloak which she hands to* PEG *later in the scene.*

MRS GARNER. Quick! It's the King, sir – the King is coming round –

FOOTE. Oh – so he graces us now, does he? – well, I have no intention of standing for the man whose wager is not paid here – personally I blame the parents – King my arse –

FRANK *ushers in* KING GEORGE, *looking stern, followed by* HUNTER.

GARRICK/PEG/MRS GARNER. Your Majesty.

KING GEORGE. Mrs Woffington, Mr Garrick, Mr Foote.

GARRICK. Your presence does the theatre great honour, sir... we were hoping of course that the Lord Chamberlain would approve this... display of British... pluck.

PEG. Mr Foote was just saying, in truth, how much he admires... your person.

KING GEORGE. Yes I heard. Mr Foote; some jests, they say, outlive the jester. The Lame Lover – what what! What what! The Lord Chamberlain tells me this should be banned. This, he was telling me, this is the opposite of comedy – so I told him what you told me – do you recall?

FOOTE. No, sir.

KING GEORGE. You told me once the opposite of comedy…
is Germany. I can't say I understood. But I think we ought to
take the British approach – the army will want to strike you a
medal!

HUNTER. Wondrous brave, Foote. Fearless.

KING GEORGE. I was saying just the other day, to the Queen,
'If only there were a way, if only, to make amends – poor
Foote, that horse of mine' – and yet you have – you have
triumphed over our poor joke –

FOOTE. There is a way actually, Your Majesty.

KING GEORGE. What what?

FOOTE. A Theatre Royal licence.

KING GEORGE. What?

GARRICK. What?!

PEG. What?

FOOTE. What what exactly. That's the amends I ask. And not a
leg too soon. 'Theatre Royal, Haymarket' I was thinking, has
a certain ring to it – a Theatre Royal of comedy, sir – as the
settling of a king's bad debt…

KING GEORGE. I – er –

GARRICK. You can't.

PEG. Sammy, you can't.

KING GEORGE. I think he just did.

Scene Three

HUNTER*'s study.*

A clock ticks. HUNTER *is drying his hands.*

HUNTER. Whenever you are ready. Thank you for bringing
Mr Frank. I'd wanted a word. I watched you from the
window... coming up Jermyn Street in your sedan chair
with your blackamoor behind you – you looked like
Cleopatra...

PEG *comes out from behind a screen, doing up her cloak.
They stare at each other for a moment.*

PEG. Yes.

He motions for her to sit down.

HUNTER. It's a question of timing.

PEG. Yes.

HUNTER. It's a canker on the ovaries, Mrs Woffington.
We cannot know for sure, as the symptoms, which cause
you such discomfort, are not dissimilar at first to cysts
upon the womb.

PEG. Or indeed to being with child.

HUNTER. To begin with, yes. I am sorry. But it's gone further
now. So I believe this to be a full-blown tumour. Not very
fast growing.

PEG. I see.

HUNTER. Operations have been attempted, but without
success. When it comes to the... softer areas of humankind, I
find I am a mere barber-surgeon.

PEG. You cannot amputate a womb.

HUNTER. I cannot.

HUNTER starts writing something and preparing powders.

PEG. He isn't what he was, you know. He has such pain in the leg that is no longer there. He can't sit onstage of course – nothing bends. Wooden as a puppet. It's as if he doesn't care. It scares me, John. He doesn't care.

HUNTER. No doctor can address wanton recklessness.

PEG. No. I'll have Frank come up, then. (*Rings a bell.*) About the timing, Mr Hunter – it's so important for a comedienne –

HUNTER. Should we not, Mrs Woffington, always be prepared for the last scene?

Enter FRANK.

PEG. Frank, I think Mr Hunter has something for Mr Foote. I'll wait in the sedan. Good day, Mr Hunter – I will see you, perhaps, at my Benefit Night.

HUNTER. Always.

Exit PEG. HUNTER has both pills and also letters.

Could you take this for Mr Foote? And, Frank, might I ask you something?

FRANK. Sir.

HUNTER. To inform me if there is any sudden change.

FRANK. With Mrs Woffington?

HUNTER. With your master. Would you do that?

FRANK. I watch from the wings. I don't give notes and I don't take money.

HUNTER. No. I meant – as... a friend. Any sudden changes? You are, I believe, Mr Foote's... friend?

FRANK. Sir?

HUNTER. Being celebrated has its dangers, Mr Frank, – in London, it is like a new dis-ease. A sort of madness. You should be circumspect.

FRANK. When you have survived, Mr Foote says, you are free.

HUNTER. Does he.

HUNTER *hands* FRANK *two sealed letters as well as the powders.* FRANK *glances at the addresses.*

FRANK. For Mr Benjamin Franklin, Craven Street, and for Addisons, Longacre? The puppet makers?

HUNTER. The puppet makers.

Scene Four

Haymarket dressing room.

FOOTE *is changing into his costume as Sir Luke Limp – a sort of dandy highwayman – as he is sitting it is not immediately apparent that he is wearing his new prothesis, which looks much like a real leg held in callipers. Enter* PEG, *who conversely changes in this scene into her 'cabin boy' costume.*

MRS GARNER. Ladies and gentlemen of the Theatre Royal Haymarket Company, your half-hour call. You're late, Mrs Woffington.

PEG. Am I? How are we?

FOOTE. Well, there's the slight annoyance of the missing leg, Mrs Woffington, but on the whole rather fine today. Look at this. (*Swinging his new prosthesis leg into view.*) Messrs Hunter & Franklin & the Drury Lane Puppet Makers: a co-production. It even bends at the ankle. A little. Bookings are good for Sir Luke Limp in *The Devil on Two Sticks*. And my Romeo in *The Lame Lover*, quoth Mr Burney, is so funny he is considering cutting his own leg off. You've seen the papers? I'm trying to decide how to put in more Bickerstaffe gags. Silly bugger.

PEG. Poor Isaac.

FOOTE. Poor Isaac my arse. Caught in St James's with his pantaloons down-jiv'd and three palace guardsmen as witness... three! So, more Bickerstaffe, yes? What do you think? Frank, can I have a coffee?

PEG.... Sam, they won't laugh about Bickerstaffe.

FOOTE. Everyone knows what goes on in St James's Park.

PEG. Sam, there were witnesses; he'll hang.

FOOTE. Like I say, silly arse...

PEG. Things change; there's a war on, Sam.

FOOTE. Yes, well, bugger that – and bugger Bickerstaffe.

FRANKLIN *is entering and has overheard.*

FRANKLIN. May I intrude?

FOOTE. I'm afraid Mrs Woffington is uncharacteristically fully dressed, Mr Franklin. Come in.

FRANKLIN. Mrs Woffington, Mr Foote – at your mirrors and your maquillage – I don't mean to interrupt – I came to see my puppet-leg in action.

FOOTE. Here 'tis. Hunter credits you entirely for the design, and Mrs Woffington for revealing to him that I was already wooden anyway. Strumpet. I've two – I've ordered three more.

PEG. One for each act.

FOOTE. Can never have too many legs, Peg. And actually having them dressed for different roles saves Frank a lot of time, doesn't it?

FRANK *is entering carrying the other prosthesis, dressed with a lady's pink stocking and shoe, and he bends it in demonstrating.*

FRANK. It does. It's very life-like, Mr Franklin, 'ingenious' and I believe the word is 'articulated'.

FRANKLIN. Why thank you. I could do with some myself – Franklins on either side of the ocean – I am going to be recalled to the Americas –

PEG. Back and forth, Mr Franklin, back and forth – you seem more at sea than on land.

FRANKLIN. I am indeed. The latest terms from London will not appease the assembly in Philadelphia.

PEG. Hush! No politics! Politics are banned backstage –

FRANKLIN. No politics, Mrs Woffington. Just my congratulations. And good-luck gifts for you. (*Hands them paper kites*.) It's good to have you back on stage, Mr Foote…

FOOTE. I am cut off too now, Mr Franklin, I am… America – free to do what I like.

FRANKLIN. Even joke about Bickerstaffe?

FOOTE. Yes, well, Bickerstaffe was a fool. Would you credit there's honest British soldiers will rather play entrapment than fight revolting Americans – begging your pardon? In my day guardsmen sold their arses not their testimony. This is a free and godless city, Mr Franklin.

FRANKLIN. It has some liberties. The question is how to preserve them –

FOOTE. By laughter, Mr Franklin, and evading cant, that's the English way.

PEG. Comedy is what distinguishes us from the animal kingdom.

FOOTE. – and from the Germans.

PEG. And from the Germans.

MRS GARNER. Beginners, Mr Foote, Mrs Woffington – I am going to have to send you to your place, sir.

FRANKLIN. Quite. In science you need to test a theory. We have an experiment in democracy. Which is a sort of liberty. But I shall miss our discussions, Mr Foote, back in my puritan land – and I will miss your... liberty. Thank you for your advice on public speaking in dresses; I'll consider it for the Congress. Mrs Woffington, your servant. You should put a conducting rod on your theatre, by the way, in case of a storm.

FRANKLIN *leaves*.

FOOTE (*calling after*). If you go, can I keep your glass harmonica? Harkee, Frank – no one better at talking freedom than the drivers of slaves – arghh.

PEG. What's the matter?

FOOTE. My head – I –

PEG. Frank – Frank, quickly, Mr Hunter should be in –

FOOTE. No – it passes – I'll be fine.

Scene Five

Haymarket stage.

FOOTE *and* PEG *in* The Devil on Two Sticks. *Sir Luke Limp is a one-legged rakish gentleman highwayman, with a walking cane and the stiff false leg and Ensign Harris* (PEG, *the ingenue, Viola-as-Cesario*) *the object of his lust.*

FOOTE (*as Sir Luke Limp*). 'She is alone as I wished. Come, you rebellious colony then, come let me find your liberty, my America, my Newfoundland. Madam – '

PEG (*dressed as a captain's boy*). 'You mean, sir, sure, sir.'

FOOTE. 'I know your game, and you know mine, Ensign Harris.'

PEG (*aside*). 'I am discovered! But, sir, your infirmity, assuredly, renders us both worse than half men.'

FOOTE. 'The worse? No; much the better, my dear. To be sure, I am a little awkward at the act of love, but much the better at bed hopping. There are advantages to losing a leg, consider, I can have neither gout nor corns nor fear of being of stepped on in a dance with you – and you'll allow, madam, the blood has to go somewhere. So now let me tar and feather you in kisses and strap you to my main-mast.'

PEG. 'Oh, sir!'

FOOTE *stares blankly for a second and stumbles – he is struggling . He has dried. Silence. Pain.*

FOOTE. Oh, please.

Silence. FOOTE *grabs* PEG, *his face contorted.*

PEG.... '"Oh, please" to what? Sir Luke.'

FOOTE. The crew mistake you for a man, Mrs Woffington? AGAIN? Because there's an entire crew backstage and half the stalls here could swear on oath you're not.

Continues backstage.

PEG. What was that?

FOOTE. What?

PEG. That – that improvisation? A little ad lib is one thing, Sam, but I'd rather you didn't throw insults at me in person as well as in character. Look, you've left a bruise.

FOOTE. Don't ever presume to lecture me about the stage, Mrs Woffington, after that, your... homage to fromage.

PEG. Oh, stick your leg up your arse, Sam.

FOOTE. Would you bring round the early papers tomorrow, Mrs Garner?

MRS GARNER. You leave me out of it.

FOOTE. Shall we see what the papers make of the latest vehicle for Peg's legs. 'Mrs' Woffington, of whom there was never a 'Mr' trailing off the London stage, accoutred in her finest silks and showing off her sagging thighs, yet again, be-perfumed in her favoured scent; flaps de poisson.

PEG *slaps him, and exits.* FOOTE *clutches his head and stumbles.*

Scene Six

HUNTER*'s study – daytime.*

FOOTE *in a chair, still in his dandy highwayman costume,* HUNTER *is feeling his head, taking his pulse, checking his eyes, etc., and taking notes.*

FOOTE. My mother always said there was something wrong in my head. Never knew when a joke went too far... tied the Provost of Worcester to a cow and set fire to its tail. That didn't go down well.

HUNTER. With the Provost or the cow?

FOOTE. Neither, but it was the Provost who sent me down for moral turpitude. Do you think I am going mad?

HUNTER. You're walking around London dressed like this. It's not safe. It isn't like it was. There's a war on –

FOOTE. Why do people keep saying that?

HUNTER. What?

FOOTE. That there's a war on. As if that justifies anything. Some insurgency in a faraway land where savages slay soldiers and we grow tobacco, well, good luck to them I say, just leave me out of it. What did Peg want before the show tonight?

HUNTER. I can't talk about that.

FOOTE. Peg doesn't remember a time when she wasn't
    famous. Can you imagine? No before. Only mirrors and
    laughter. They fed her on gin until she was thirteen of
    course, keep her little, and then a pregnancy every year for
    a decade, and none as she could own... I'm writing a play
    for her, did I tell you? About the Chudleigh woman. Peg is
    dying, isn't she?

HUNTER. I think you might consider being gentler with her.
    Chudleigh? Is that wise? In the current climate? The Duchess
    has a lot of very powerful friends on Fleet Street; editors in
    her pocket, print-shop owners.

FOOTE. She's a West Country tart, and I should know. She's
    a bigamist. She'll be tried in the Lords and of course she'll
    be convicted, though it hardly matters, I appreciate,
    'because there is a war on', but yes, I thought it had the
    makings of a farce.

HUNTER. On the whole I think there's a limited appetite for
    kicking ladies when they are down –

FOOTE. Yes. I'll apologise to Peg. She does a portrait-perfect
    impersonation of the Duchess – so do I as it happens, so we
    needn't actually name her –

HUNTER. Just make sure the story doesn't switch to you.

    Enter FRANKLIN *with newspapers and box, from which he
    takes out a contraption that looks a bit like a porcupine hat.*

FRANKLIN. I came as fast as I could... I sail tonight.

FOOTE. Why on earth would you leave London?

FRANKLIN. Because it turns out I am not an Englishman after
    all, Mr Foote. I brought the cranioscoper, Jock.

FOOTE. More electricity?

FRANKLIN. It measures the tiniest details of the skull, Mr
    Foote – it is the system of mind-knowledge – *phrenos, logos,*

phrenology – I will leave it here… and the glass harmonica, Mr Foote, it's yours.

FOOTE *puts on the cranioscoper.*

HUNTER. I think I begin to understand the blockage, Sam, I think that is what is causing these seizures. After an operation, there is a clot in the blood and it can move. And sometimes, we know, this stops the heart. Sometimes, it stops the brain, or part of it, and we see people half-imbeciled. With you –

FRANKLIN. With you, Hunter thinks he has found a permanent lodged blockage – fascinating – affecting more of the brain…

HUNTER. It is the sideways, darkened view we have – where we study the mind from, Mr Foote, from the wings.

FRANKLIN. Our perspective on perception – it's like the Atlantic before Colombus.

HUNTER. But because of that, we study people who are missing things.

FOOTE. Oh – my leg.

HUNTER. No. Your inhibition.

Scene Seven

Haymarket dressing room and stage.

FRANK *and* FOOTE *rehearsing.* FRANK *has a copy of the
play open that he can glance at.* FOOTE *is changed by* FRANK
from Sir Luke Limp into drag as Mrs Cole in The Minor – MRS
GARNER *is in and out, bringing him his costume and wig.*

FOOTE (*as Mrs Cole the bawd in* The Minor). ' – but Dr
Wesley has turned my brain' – is there a line there, Frank?

FRANK. No – you're right so far – shall I heat water for a bath
while we're doing this?

FOOTE. Maybe later. 'Oh but Dr Wesley has turned my brain –
there had I been, a tossing over a sea of sin – '

MRS GARNER. You can't say that.

FOOTE. Watch me. Wesley? Hypocritical ham – where was I?

FRANK. Tossing yourself over a sea of sin. The Wesleyans are
Abolitionists, you know –

FOOTE. The virtuous are ridiculous too, Frank. 'Young
reverend, if your mind be set upon a country virgin for
tomorrow night I believe I can furnish you with one who will
like your back-alley ways.'

FRANK. You can't say 'back-alley ways'. And you can't attack
the church like this –

FOOTE. I'll say what I want as I long as I can learn it.

Onstage, continuous.

'Sixteen years I have toiled as whoremistress and as it says
outside our Covent Garden brothel: 'No papists, no
Americans, no credit' – my girls are patriots, so why do

people wonder at my Wesleyan conversion? Well, there's method in my madness – a new birth, a rebirth, and I have become, as you see, a complete and born-again, degenerate woman.'

Scene continues back in the Haymarket dressing room.

The offstage bed is now more centre stage, PEG *is in it, under covers and not visible at first.* GARRICK *storms in.*

GARRICK. What the hell was that, Sammy? What the fuck do you think you are doing? I had the Lord Chamberlain in at Drury Lane, he left at the second interval because, and I quote 'Mr Foote was said to be impersonating Dr Wesley, profaning the Lord, criticising politicians and newspaper editors while dressed as a whoremonger.' There are rumours in every gazette, Sam – they built us up, they can tear us down. Are you out of your periwigged mind?

FOOTE. Good evening, Davy.

GARRICK. Have you any idea how hard we are battling to keep the Licensing Act from being extended? Mrs Garrick is daily inviting bishops to tea, and we've had to set up a Society for the Relief of Distressed Actresses – DON'T – and you blaspheme, on stage, dressed as a common whore.

FOOTE. I wouldn't say common exactly –

GARRICK. Peg – Peg, I know you are there – knock some sense into him, can't you? We cannot talk about religion, we cannot impersonate known and clear personages, we never attack the press, or they attack us, and we cannot, cannot, CANNOT allude, so directly, to... carnal knowledge... let alone the wholesale whoremongering of the whoremonger-general.

FOOTE. Oh, keep your wig on, Davy – it's my theatre and it's my best joke. The theatre is a knocking shop, Davy, always was and always will be – it is the pulling back of the curtains, to reveal the nakedness beneath... that's what theatre means.

PEG. Don't fight, boys, please, not now.

> FRANK *has entered with hot water into which* PEG *puts her feet. He tenderly washes her feet and remakes the bed during:*

GARRICK. Peg, are you all right? –

FOOTE. Charge us with vagrancy laws – go on – do we care? We don't do tragedy at the Haymarket, we don't do Shakespeare any more and we don't do Metastasian Italian operas by George Fuckric Handel – we do men in skirts and girls in pants while women in the front boxes have sex with footmen. This is England.

FRANK. Do they?

FOOTE. Have sex? It's not obligatory, obviously, Frank, some people do watch the play – the Queen for instance.

PEG (*hoarsely*). Why do you think their bosoms heave so?

FOOTE. Is it laughter? Is the workings of Mrs Woffington's art or of their corsetry? Bollocks. That's what it is. Why, the Countess of Northumberland came twice during my epilogue last night and practically warranted applause for her efforts –

PEG. Or his.

FOOTE. Or his.

GARRICK. Dear God.

FOOTE. God has nothing to do with it – you can watch her from the wings, Frank, if you like –

PEG. She's very good, I'm told.

FOOTE. Leans over the railings for the better view.

PEG. Or better angle.

FOOTE. I hadn't thought of that. What a paragon of the peerage she is – so don't ever think it's far away, Davy, nor should it be – in my theatre you are always as near to a rat as you are to a well-fingered fanny, and sometimes it's the one doing the other.

PEG. Hear, hear!

FOOTE. What is our entry in Sam Johnson's Dictionary, Peg: The Theatre.

PEG. 'An erotic act by candlelight.'

FOOTE. An erotic act by candlelight, Davy. That is what it means.

GARRICK. Well, if that were true there wouldn't be so much laughter would there?

PEG. You should get about more, Davy.

She collapses, coughing.

GARRICK. Peg, I'm sorry – what curs we are; arguing around my lady's bedchamber.

PEG. Thank you, darling. Tell us a story, Sammy. Cheer me up.

GARRICK (*half-whispered*). Dear God, man – how long has she been like this?

FOOTE. Frank – I think you'd better go for Mr Hunter.

FRANK *exits.* FOOTE *takes* MRS COLE'*s shawl and wraps it round* PEG *as he talks. His wig and maybe his dress is all off by now.*

You lay there. Davy and I are going to hop on the bed. This may take some time – as the uniped said to the actress. Now did I tell you, I was walking down the Haymarket yesterday – I say walking, obviously I was mainly being carried in m'sedan chair – but it makes for a better start for the story – you sit there, Davy, I was walking down the Haymarket, when who should I see but your Lord Sandwich, cramming something awful-looking into his mouth. 'What ho, Foote', quoth he – as I stepped out towards m'theatre, minding my own business – 'What's this we hear of your being a bugger? When will I receive what you owe me – for truly, sir, from

what I hear, I don't know whether you shall die on the
gallows or of the pox.' 'That rather depends, my lord,' I
replied, 'on whether I embrace your principles or your
mistress.'

PEG. Ha – very good – what did he say?

FOOTE. Damn him if he didn't opine that I had an insufficiency
of legs to attempt his mistress, and a superfluity of legs to be
hung straight.

PEG. Damn his eyes.

FOOTE. Exactly and damn him if he didn't take notes – pencil
and paper – and tell me he was going to use it all at the
Beefsteak that night stealing my jokes!

PEG. Sue if he does.

FOOTE. So I shall. So I shall...

GARRICK (*plumps up pillows and sings, from* Twelfth Night).
    'Trip no further pretty sweeting
    Journeys end in lovers meeting.'

FOOTE. My mother. My mother was not best pleased, I feel, as
a lady of discernment, with what she had wrought in a son.
No; shh. And my world has been the theatre and... the
occasional military skirmish... you have been a touch of
watered satin... my true friend... and there is no finer thing a
harsh critic can say.

PEG. Ah sure, you're an old fraud, Sammy. Can you top that
now, Mr Garrick?

GARRICK. I cannot.

PEG. You were always useless without a script, Davy.

    'That very time I saw you... a certain aim he took
    At a fair vestal...

She signs 'I love you' the old-stage way.

    As it should pierce a hundred thousand hearts... but it
        took mine...'

GARRICK. You weren't such a vestal.

PEG. Oh course I feckin' wasn't – (*To* GARRICK.) see, I
always intended, Davy, to play tragedy with you again –

FOOTE. Well, I don't think we can bill it as tragedy with three-
in-a-bed.

PEG. No. My boys. I was thinking, if you could leave anything
– tho' it'll be nice to peek out of a sly canvas from time to
time, tits and eyes – if you could leave anything, really
worthwhile, though you'd never be remembered for it, I was
thinking, wouldn't it be good, on a stage, to leave the sound
of laughter?

Scene Eight

Haymarket dressing room and stage.

FRANK *enters with* FOOTE*'s 'Duchess' overdress.* FOOTE *is
sitting at* PEG*'s dressing table.* MRS GARNER *enters and she
and* FRANK *exchange glances.*

MRS GARNER. Beginners, Mr Foote.

FOOTE. Thank you. Frank?

FRANK *takes from* PEG*'s dressing table the 'Duchess' wig
with the Chudleigh feather. It is apparent that* PEG *is not
there.*

FOOTE *seems very unsteady.*

The first part of his breakdown speech may be FOOTE
rehearsing in PEG*'s mirror… then onstage. He manhandles
his fake leg under his skirt, moving with difficulty and pain.*

(*Dressed as the Duchess in* The Trip to Calais.) A lady of a
certain age advertised in the *Westminster Gazette* in want of
a lover with the amorous powers of Hercules. When her
doorbell chain was pulled, she found by her boot-scraper a

soldier, sans arms, sans legs, and when she asked him 'What are you doing here?', he answered, 'Madam, I am responding to your advertisement for a lover.' Quoth the lady: 'Well, how did you imagine this would go?' Quoth the soldier, 'Well, how do you imagine I pulled the door bell?' Keep staring, I might do a trick. Heard the one about the comedian with one leg called Foote? What's his other leg called? Heard the one about the depeditation of Mr Foote? The wit? Well, it's half-true. The thing is, you just have to take it on the chin, amputation. I do appreciate it's not easy to heckle a one-legged comedian. Gentlefolk are embarrassed. Don't be. Though the best heckle I ever had was here at the Haymarket from a blind man, he said 'Get off... has he gone yet?' And Lord but it's a conversation starter – having no leg. People ask me how I take it off. But I *know* what they mean. Sometimes ladies even ask me outright, they say: can you have carnal relations? And I say: Madam, does your husband usually take a run-up? So I can't really complain when people stop and stare *now*, can I? Now that the Duchess calls me a sodomite.

He appears to be having some sort of seizure. MRS GARNER *and* FRANK *can be glimpsed on the gantry – she sends* FRANK *off (for* HUNTER *and* GARRICK) *and then can be seen signalling to the orchestra.*

Children stare a lot. So I tell them to FUCK OFF, they can't afford the theatre anyway. But if I really want to be alone, I tell gentlefolk we can either talk about amputee erotica or my new relationship with Jesus.

The orchestra begins to drown him out.

I'm sorry. Where was I? Dying on stage. You see this was meant to be Peggy's role. The late Mrs Woffington. Loses her celebrated sense of timing.

He clutches his head and cries out in pain.

Go home? Why would I go home? This is home.

The sound of a storm approaching. And booing.

Scene Nine

The roof of the Haymarket Theatre.

Behind the pediment on the roof. The back of a royal crest is visible. And some of London's skyline. The sound of a storm, moving nearer. FOOTE *on a precipice, still in drag but wigless and with a kite. Enter* FRANK *with* GARRICK.

FRANK. He's up here, sir.

GARRICK. What are you doing, Sam?

FOOTE. Came to fly a kite.

GARRICK. Come down, Sam – it's not safe.

FOOTE. The best views aren't, Davy. Franklin's idea; kites in bad weather; but he's right on most things. Apart from the glass harmonica obviously.

GARRICK. You need to come down. There's going to be a storm...

FOOTE. Macklin used to say, do you remember, Macklin used to say you'd be forgiven anything for a great finale. You can be everything all evening, but if you don't get them in the closing act, you're sunk. Like Lear – no decent jokes with the daughter, mad old fucker – such a downer.

GARRICK. You need to come down...

FOOTE. We're going to put one of Mr Franklin's conductors on the top here, just over the royal crest. Look, Davy – King of Comedy! I could jump, now that really would make for a finale –

FRANK. Come down, please, sir, Let me help.

FOOTE. No, I am staying up here. Tell Mr Hunter I've found the perfect place for the new lightning conductor!

FRANK. I can go for Mr Hunter – do you want me to go, sir?

GARRICK. I'll stay here with him, Frank. You go.

FRANK. I'll go then, shall I?

GARRICK. Even if Hunter is operating.

Exit FRANK.

The Lord Chamberlain suggested I take off *Midsummer Night's Dream,* too many faeries, and put on *The Wars of the Roses.* You need to, maybe go away for a while, Sam.

FOOTE. Why would she go? Now? I don't know why she had to go –

GARRICK. No… I'm not sure you playing the Duchess is the wisest epitaph for Peg just now, Sammy. I think the Duchess will sue.

FOOTE. Oh, it's much worse than that. Chudleigh has written to the *Westminster Gazette*, about me and Frank. Saying I am a sodomite.

GARRICK. Jesus. And they're printing?

FOOTE. Well, not pictures obviously. It's advertised tomorrow: A new play about Mr Foote for the Haymarket: *Sodom and Onan.*

GARRICK. If they are printing they must have her affidavit and her money to do it. This is a disaster. Well, you must sue. There's no evidence. Is there?

FOOTE. For the sodomy or the onanism?

GARRICK. Dear God alive, man, why, WHY when you are on the very precipice, do you skip at life like it matters to no one? Stop. Desist. Quip your last. We are here – who want you to come down. At least have respect for those of us who love you, the storm can kill you.

FOOTE. The storm's passing.

GARRICK. It was a *metaphor*, man –

FOOTE. No lightning bolts. No operatics. I promise. Will you stay here a while with me, till Hunter gets here?

GARRICK. I said I would.

FOOTE. What's the answer, Davy, for the one-legged comedian on the precipice? When I hear laughter, I know there is something rubbing against what they once thought was right. That's what I do. I annoy. And people laugh, and sometimes – not often but sometimes – someone thinks a little differently because they have laughed in a theatre, at a man in a dress, when they might have thrown bricks.

HUNTER *has climbed up and heard some of the above.*

HUNTER. What the hell are you two doing up here?

FOOTE. Rehearsing – the rain it raineth – *Lear the Comedy* – it's a sort of sequel.

GARRICK. We are coming down.

HUNTER. There are crowds at the stage door, Sam – there's a rumour you are going to be arrested.

GARRICK. It's not true. There's no evidence. I'll go down and see if I can persuade them to make trouble elsewhere. (*Starts to go.*) Peg said it was only you who made her feel alive on stage – because she never knew what you were going to do next.

FOOTE. Nor do I generally.

GARRICK. Franklin told me there's this place where Mr Newton's gravities cancel each other out – did you know that? Some point nearer the moon than here. He'd worked it out mathematically – this is right isn't it, John? Anyway, he said this place – if you had a *thought*, it might flutter for ever; a 'pulse' of his 'electric fluid' that can't go anywhere. Imagine. Like in a theatre – the mind – it's floating, somewhere above the stalls where there's no gravity. Me.

My words – Shakespeare's – Sammy's. The audience. And
the meaning floats. Maybe for ever. All that training,
Sammy, so we can forget everything. And be forgotten…
The one-legged comedian on the edge; I think the answer is
to walk very carefully. There's no evidence. Sue her. The
press hate the Duchess and the audience loves you. Lie. It's
what we do.

Exit GARRICK.

HUNTER. I have opiates.

FOOTE. It's not the pain, not really. It's the desire to jump over
– the footlights – do something unconscionable. Not give a
damn. It has become – constant.

Exit FOOTE.

HUNTER (*addresses audience as a lecture*). We are men of
science, and we anatomise bodies without sentiment; and in
so doing we find the famous and the dead share this: we are
most fascinated in them when they are about to decompose
before us. The celebrated can be as instructive as the
departed: it is a founding principle of the study of humanity,
and of the mind, that we must acknowledge how we are
different, in order to know properly what we share.

Scene Ten

Haymarket dressing room.

FRANK *is preparing shaving tackle. Noise of a building site in the background.* MRS GARNER *enters in a flap.*

MRS GARNER. Frank! Frank, where are you?

FRANK. I'm here, Mrs G – calm down.

MRS GARNER. I'll calm down when we're all dead, Mr Frank, which is looking rather sooner than not – how is he? No – I don't want to know – what's that infernal knocking?

FRANK. Benches in the gallery and reinforcing the footlights railings.

MRS GARNER. Oh, sweet heavens. There's going to be a riot – I can feel it my waters –

FRANK. Have you done the Act Two wig?

MRS GARNER. He's not going on as the Duchess again?

FRANK. It has been advertised, yes, and the new one about the buggering monk.

MRS GARNER. Well, that puts me back on the streets within a week and a theatre in tatters.

FRANK. All will be well, Mrs G. He hasn't had a seizure again, and the Duchess can't reprint her accusation for fear of libel.

MRS GARNER. Well, she can say anything on trial in the Lords for bigamy – and it doesn't bear thinking about what mud she could fling – or who might be called. So why goad her?

Enter FOOTE.

FOOTE. Why goad who, Mrs Garner?

MRS GARNER. I'm sorry, sir. The Duchess, sir.

FOOTE. We've never worried about the critics, Mrs Garner, I am not going to start now. We haven't really a leg for a monk have we, Frank?

FRANK. No, sir – how about the Luke Limp?

FOOTE. What do you think, Mrs Garner? Do monks wear stockings? Frank and I will bow to your superior knowledge of men's undergarments.

MRS GARNER. Heaven preserve us.

Exit MRS GARNER. FRANK *prepares* FOOTE *for shaving.*

FRANK. I met your friend Dr Johnson last night. Said I should borrow from his library if I've read all your cabinet of plays. Which I have.

FOOTE. Old curmudgeon. What's he suggesting you read? Him on Shakespeare I suppose –

FRANK. *Tristram Shandy.*

FOOTE. Nine volumes in search of a joke, Frank, I thought I kept you busier.

FRANK. And that I should leave your employ.

FOOTE. Did he. Might be wise. He's wanting help with his dictionary, Frank – or are you asking for a raise?

FRANK. No, Mr Foote, sir. This my home. Shall we do those lines from *The Duchess*?

FOOTE. Very well. Come here.

FRANK. That's not the line.

FOOTE. No – come here.

FRANK. Do you want me to change the leg, Mr Foote?

FOOTE. When you looked after your young master – over the seas – did you shave him?

FRANK. What? Yes. Of course.

FOOTE. You must have sometimes been tempted.

FRANK. Sir?

FOOTE. With only half an inch of cut-throat razor between you and retribution?

FRANK. I don't – I don't like to think about those times. I think of it, like a bad tragedy that got taken off. Locked in the cabinet. Do you want me to change the leg dressing, Mr Foote, while we do the lines?

FOOTE. I want you to come here. Here. Take your shirt off.

FRANK. What?

FOOTE. It's a dressing room. Take your shirt off. You see me – this – all the time. This great lump of ham. I've never seen you –

FRANK. Please. Mr Foote. I – I can fetch Mr Hunter – I –

FOOTE. Show me… if you love me.

FRANK *slowly takes off his shirt. He picks up the razor and goes as if to continue shaving, shirtless. His back is scarred. He is in front of* FOOTE *with the razor.* FOOTE *touches* FRANK *–* FOOTE *is shaking, the beginnings of a seizure.*

FRANK. Mr Foote – sir. Please. Please. I – Mrs Garner will come back any second and –

FOOTE. I want to have a fuck at you. Like you and your young master.

FRANK. You're not well. What we did… what he did… please… it cannot be named… I –

FOOTE. No words. You told me. St James's Park. I don't want pity.

FRANK. Mr Foote. Please. Not like this. You're hurting me. Mr Foote.

FOOTE *pulls him down and kisses him.* FRANK *holds up
the cut-throat razor, high above them, his arm shaking. But
they kiss.*

Scene Eleven

FOOTE*'s nightmare. Various Londons:* HUNTER*'s study/Drury
Lane/Haymarket dressing room.*

*We see, as we have before, the 'onstage' and 'offstage' but now,
a quintet of interrelated Londons that may also be in* FOOTE*'s
disturbed mind and in a real or 'stage' storm – orchestrated and
stage-managed by* MRS GARNER. HUNTER *is rehearsing his
lecture with notes later taken by* MRS GARNER. HUNTER *is
interrupted at this by* FRANK. GARRICK *is onstage as Lear
with Cordelia –* (*in* FOOTE*'s mind she is* PEG). *Later we even
see* FRANKLIN *reading* HUNTER*'s lecture. Perhaps* FOOTE
*wanders between the scenes, as in a dream. Handel music
underscores.*

FOOTE (*as if at a stage door, scribbling a pencilled note*). Can
you tell Mr Garrick that Mr Foote is here? I am looking for
Frank Barber. The Black boy from the Haymarket. I thought
he might have come here. Has he come through stage door?

PEG/CORDELIA. Sir, do you not know me?

GARRICK/KING LEAR.
'You are a spirit, I know: when did you die?
Where have you been?'

FOOTE. Peg. Peg, is that you? I'm not in my right mind, Peg
and –

GARRICK/KING LEAR.
'Thou art a soul in bliss; but I am bound
Upon a wheel of fire, that mine own tears
Do scald like moulten lead.

Where am I?
I am mightily abused... You do me wrong to take me out
     o' the grave.'

FOOTE. I am not mad, Peg – I have to tell Frank – he's run
away you see and –

PEG/CORDELIA.
     'O you kind gods,
     Cure this great breach in his abused nature!
                              Restoration hang
     Thy medicine on my lips; and let this kiss
     Repair these violent harms.'

FOOTE. I don't know this scene, Peg, the Fool isn't in it... Peg,
can you hear me?

HUNTER. The anatomising of the celebrated should also be
the work of men of reason – like the stars in heaven, we
learn most from them as they fall, when we and they
become conscious that they are constructed by the
perception of others.

FOOTE. I'll leave a note for Mr Garrick then, for when he is
offstage. Please give this to him. It's very important.

PEG/CORDELIA (*while handing old Lear his clothes*).
     '...O, look upon me, sir,
     And hold your hands in benediction o'er me:
     No, sir, you must not kneel...'

FRANK *is kneeling at* MRS GARNER*'s feet. She hands him
his shirt and clothes.*

MRS GARNER. Stand up. Frank. Stand up and you be a man.
They live by other rules. We pity and admire. Don't be
destroyed by it. You could go to sea – you... we're different,
you and me. It's all very well in plays, doxies and dandies –
larks in the piazza. I worked these streets so I know, Frank. I
see everything, Frank; slavery comes in many colours.

FRANK. You watch, Mrs Garner. You don't ever see. I have
my name and I have free will and that is all – I will not be
owned.

MRS GARNER (*composes herself and closes the razor and gives it back to him and touches his cheek*). No. What are you going to do?

HUNTER. We find the price we pay for our free will and consciousness is the price of knowing what pleasure is, and what love is, and knowing also when it is missing, or unattainable, or lost.

FOOTE. I'd like to place an advertisement please, one of our servants, one of my friends – I want it to say that if he returns he will be treated fairly. No – no he didn't steal anything. Black, yes. A blackamoor. No; he was a slave but he is free. He is a free man.

FRANK *stands by* HUNTER*'s desk.*

HUNTER. And when he did this, he seemed freely conscious of what he was doing? This is important.

FRANK. I've said. I've told you. I have declared what he is.

HUNTER. I wish you had not. Mr Barber. You should not have said.

FRANK. I have nowhere. Do you understand? He doesn't own me. I could have gone to Justice Fielding.

HUNTER. Indeed.

FRANK. You told me to tell you if there was any violent change in his behaviour –

HUNTER. You should not have said the words, Frank. You should not have said anything that you would not have heard in a court of law. I've already been summoned to testify in the trial of the Duchess, Frank – do you not understand? They have summoned me. But they will ask about Foote.

Sound of raging storm or perhaps MRS GARNER *and* STAGE HANDS *with thunder boards on the gantry.* FOOTE *again wanders as if onto stage with Lear/Cordelia, mouthing Lear's words.*

GARRICK/KING LEAR.
> 'Pray, do not mock me:
> I am a very foolish fond old man,
> And, to deal plainly,
> I fear I am not in my perfect mind.'

FOOTE. Please, please, DO NOT LAUGH AT ME! Please, Frank, please.

PEG/CORDELIA.
> And so I am, I am.

GARRICK/KING LEAR.
> If you have poison for me, I will drink it.
> I know you do not love me:
> You have some cause.

PEG/CORDELIA.
> No cause, no cause.

> *MRS GARNER has handed HUNTER a dress coat, and taken the notes from his desk. Her usual bustle of books and notes…*

HUNTER.…the theatre of the human mind derives from an ill-lit consciousness, that we do not understand, that we watch only from the wings. And our knowledge of it is gained haphazardly, in scenes stage-managed by forces we do not comprehend, though some call this puppetry the work of God –

> *Both FOOTE and FRANKLIN are given copies of the HUNTER notes by MRS GARNER who then hands a Bible to HUNTER who stands, his hand up, swearing on oath, as witness in court. She then stands in tableau with FRANK at her feet as mirror to Lear with Cordelia. It appears to be raining.*

FRANKLIN. 'And where in the course of human events we put faith in God or science to explain how our consciousness is constructed, we may then begin to construct conscience in an age of reason.'

HUNTER (*hand on Bible as if in court*). '...the whole truth, so help me God.'

FRANKLIN. 'Freedom and free will have their price.'

FOOTE. 'The cost of our enlightenment is the loss of our innocence. We do not know we have a mind until we begin to lose it.'

A sound of heavier rain and smashing glass.

Scene Twelve

The Haymarket dressing room.

From time to time there is an explosion of sound – an angry crowd – it's not clear if it is from front of house, or behind the theatre. The sound of smashing glass and a storm.

FOOTE *enters with papers and prints. Composed again.*

MRS GARNER. Angels and ministers of grace defend us.

FOOTE. Yes. I thought I'd get here early. If nothing else my uncles taught me to be on time for an execution.

MRS GARNER. Oh, Mr Foote –

FOOTE. It's one thing to have unnameable crimes whispered in coffee shops, Mrs G, it's another thing to have them named in the House of Lords. By a friend.

MRS GARNER. Will they come for you here? Will they arrest Frank?

FOOTE. I don't think so. I think they'll hope I'll hop off. If I don't... It's odd... the crime they may not name in court is shouted by barrow boys. Frank's too. 'Roger the footman' they call him. It's a relief in some regards. The world turns. The theatre is still open. America is still revolting. They're saying this is what happens if gentlefolk don't employ proper English valets; you've got to love the *Westminster Gazette*.

MRS GARNER. What are you going to do on stage?

FOOTE. Just 'stand-up' – I thought that would be enough of a challenge today. I believe most of the company are pleading illness. Have you seen him?

MRS GARNER (*shakes her head*). Mr Bickerstaffe ran away. To Paris. Join him. Parisian landladies must be triple-booked with English sodomites –

FOOTE. Yes thank you, Mrs Garner. Did he leave word, at all?

MRS GARNER *shakes her head*.

It's just I left him a note. It wasn't his fault, you know? He named me to Hunter. He thought he was doing right. Hunter names me in court. I am named.

MRS GARNER. You are un-named. You are destroyed, and us with you –

Enter FRANK. *He carries the razor, opened.*

FRANK. Mr Foote.

There is a pause, and a sudden aggressive shouting and another smashed window.

MRS GARNER. I'll go and see what's happening.

Exit MRS GARNER.

FRANK. I came to give you this. (*The razor.*) I wouldn't want to be accused of stealing. Have you seen the papers?

FOOTE. It's like a storm, Frank. It rages. It passes. Trees are felled.

FRANK. Not about you, Old Fool. Mr Franklin has signed the Declaration – that America is free. Just 'declared' it. Which is more than his slaves ever managed.

FOOTE. Declaring it is what it takes, Frank.

FRANK. They are calling me 'Roger'. (*Signalling the papers.*) 'Roger the Footman.'

FOOTE. Yes, well, you mustn't look for accuracy in the London papers…

FRANK. Stop. I've been reading and I've been thinking. I came to say… I came to say that I am not sorry for what I've said. I've named you. And I am not sorry. That's what I came to say. Mrs Woffington said she forgave Mr Garrick everything, when she saw him, out there. I don't. But I choose to be here wit' you.

FOOTE. I had hoped, before I die – not tonight on stage I mean, but die die, which must be so much less painful than dying on stage I always think – I'd like to think that someone might really know me, my nature and my name –

FRANK. I know you.

FOOTE. 'If you have poison for me, I would drink it… You have some cause' –

FRANK. 'No cause, no cause', Mr Foote .

FRANK *signals 'I love you' in the unspoken gesture taught by* PEG *but before* FOOTE *can respond:*

MRS GARNER (*running in, out of breath*). Oh, sir – you'll never believe it, sir –

FOOTE. Mrs Garner, Mr Frank has both ruined and returned to me; you cannot surprise or upstage me now.

MRS GARNER. It's the King – sir – front of house are laying out the royal box, sir –

FOOTE. Good God. Today. What what. Frank – if you're staying, the royal command performance leg I think – and champagne.

FRANK. At the half?

FOOTE. Yes, well, fuck that – it's not every day you get called a sodomite in the House of Lords and visited by

God's Anointed… I'd say it's a red-letter day all in all,
wouldn't you?

FRANK. I'll get glasses. If only Mrs Woffington were here, sir,
to see this.

FOOTE. Yes.

FRANK. There can be no theatre riot now, he is showing his
loyalty, you'll be safe – don't you think?

Exit FRANK.

FOOTE. Now don't fret, Mrs G. Have you seen the cartoons?
One-legged buggery has given young Mr Rowlandson much
merriment in his prints – have you seen them?

MRS GARNER. No.

FOOTE. Bugger or buggeree, Mrs G? What is it possible to be
with one leg? 'A feat of unipedular balance' – that's rather
good – oh, but look you should see this, it's very funny: 'Mr
Foote evades the problem of life's fifth act by not having
one'. And look: 'Sodomite!' quoth Mr Foote, 'Sodomite: I'll
not stand for it!' How do you think I am doing?

MRS GARNER. Like a man with as many legs as he needs,
Mr Foote. Please. There are horses we can hire at the
bottom of Suffolk Street. Frank and I can pack everything,
during the overture – you could be in France by this time
tomorrow and no one would think the lesser of you. No one
would. I wouldn't.

FOOTE. Really? Well well. The Haymarket, you know, it's a
Theatre Royal in my name only? I did it – a Theatre Royal
of Comedy – only three Theatres Royal, ever, and one in
My Name.

MRS GARNER. Oh. Is that right. Well, that's the celebrated Mr
Foote all over. Do you know who I saw on Piccadilly in the
storm yesterday? Your wife. Mrs Foote, as once was, failed
actress, failed wife, and I thought, I thought: 'I've watched
him from the wings every night for twenty years, and

cleaned his underwear and mopped up his blood; I'm the wife in the wings. Me.' You think it's about you on stage, but it's not, actually. I think every theatre has ghosts. Certainly this one. And every last fucking one of them was in stage management. Ignored and unthanked and uncreditted and washing other people's gussets; it's like a career in all the very worst bits of being married. And I thought, what will I be remembered for? Me? Martha to his Messiah, handmaid to his godhead? And there are many many rooms in my father's house, the Haymarket, and not one of them ever had *my* name on. So save yourself, Sammy, because you'll be forgotten anyway, like me, because I do suspect the hell awaiting actors is an eternity having to wash the socks of stage management.

Enter FRANK.

FRANK. Mr Foote – the King is coming round.

FOOTE. Right. Very well – quickly, help me up.

MRS GARNER *and* FRANK *help* FOOTE *up*.

MRS GARNER. It's past the five, Mr Foote, but we'll hold the house... of course.

KING GEORGE *enters, again in riding coat, clearly not staying*.

FOOTE. Your Majesty.

MRS GARNER *and* FRANK *leave, but leaving the door open*.

KING GEORGE. We thought you might not be here.

FOOTE. Yes, well, Garrick's not so good in a skirt really, and Lord but Handel's dull –

KING GEORGE. We have always wondered, Mr Foote, at your facility in laughing at adversity.

FOOTE. Yes, well, what else to be done with it, sir?

KING GEORGE. Such roister-doister, Mr Foote. Men in dresses. Not really the thing for our times. Losing America for the sake of a petticoat –

FOOTE. It's the papers, not the people. If you stayed, sir –

KING GEORGE. 'Presume not that I am the thing I was, old man.' They are calling it a Declaration of Independence; don't go thinking you can do the same thing. This is a storm of the Fourth Estate, Mr Foote. About you. And we need the papers to pay accord. To America. It's madness to squander such an empire, while the London papers piffle on the Chudleigh woman and you – we will not lose America for the sake of a petticoat. A nation at war makes sacrifices, Mr Foote. People lose liberties. You need to go away. Maybe the guardsmen won't actually stone you, tonight, as we have been here. But they will. And they must. You'd be mad to make a stand.

FOOTE. I am not mad. Hunter says I am just perceived as mad, maybe because of something in my brain, maybe something to do with being 'celebrated'. But I need to be seen – is that a sort of madness?

KING GEORGE. Well, that would make all kings mad, would it not? Being 'celebrated' is not the same as fame, Mr Foote – therein lies the death of kings. I see I am wasting my time.

A sudden crashing noise – breaking glass – FRANK pops his head round the corner.

FRANK. Shall I tell the orchestra to play the National Anthem, Mr Foote?

KING GEORGE. Yes do. I'll not stay. I cannot... A prince, you see, is no more a writer of his own play than any other man. Less so. If you go now, you can save yourself... that's all I came to say. If you go on, it's a declaration; they'll arrest you and you'll hang. (*Starts to go.*) Maybe we'll keep a Theatre Royal here. But not in your name. God save you...

FOOTE. Yes. And God save you, sir.

KING GEORGE. What? Yes. God save me.

Exit KING GEORGE.

MRS GARNER. If you are going to go on, Mr Foote, I don't think you can leave it any longer. Which costume?

FOOTE. I'll think I'll go on as I am. We wouldn't want them to think I went without trying to get the last laugh now, would we. Frank, can you go front of house and check when the royal party has gone. I think, I believe it would be tactful for me to wait for that, before I go on.

FRANK. Yes. I think you should do it. Shout who you are, centre stage. Be mad. It's what Mrs Woffington would do. I think they'll raise the rafters with their cheering.

FOOTE. Do you think so?

FRANK. Just declare it – it's all it takes.

FRANK *exits*.

FOOTE. Thank you for your advice, Mrs G. No laughs in posterity. There is nothing more piercing to the heart or humanising of the mind than a life in the theatre. 'Just declare it.' This is novel –

MRS GARNER. What?

FOOTE. Paying a debt, Mrs G. I think I owe Mr Frank – don't you think – rather late in my career, it might be enlightening, to declare myself; our revels now being ended... our actors... all melted into air, into thin air...

MRS GARNER. 'Leaving not a rack behind.'

FOOTE. You'll look out for young Frank? I've asked Johnson to keep an eye on him as well, but it may not be easy, if people know... his name.

MRS GARNER. Yes, Mr Foote. Best foot forward.

FOOTE. What? Right. Absolutely. See you on the other side –

And he heads upstage, the tap of his wooden leg amplified.

FRANK *returns, but* FOOTE *is already onstage. As he shuffles into position, he signals to* FRANK (*or is to the audience?*) *the wordless 'I love you' taught to them by* PEG. *It is* FOOTE *as he was at the beginning of the play.*

End.

www.nickhernbooks.co.uk

facebook.com/nickhernbooks

twitter.com/nickhernbooks